MAKING WORK

OPTIONAL

MAKING WORK OPTIONAL

Jay Kelly
C. Lenny Henderson, CFP™
Jeremy B. Johnson, , CFP™

BENBELLA

Dallas, Texas

BenBella Books
6440 N. Central Expressway
Suite 508
Dallas, TX 75206

BENBELLA

Send feedback to feedback@benbellabooks.com
www.benbellabooks.com
Printed in the United States of America

10 9 8 7 6 5 4 3 2 1

Henderson, C. Lenny.

Making work optional : a practical guide to personal and financial freedom / by C. Lenny Henderson, Jay M. Kelly, and Jeremy B. Johnson.

   p. cm.

Includes bibliographical references and index.

 ISBN 1-932100-14-8

 1. Finance, Personal. I. Kelly, Jay M. II. Johnson, Jeremy B. III.
Title.

HG179.H39 2003

 332.024'01--dc22

                        2003026678

Cover and interior design by Melody Cadungog

Distributed by Independent Publishers Group
To order call (800) 888-4741
www.ipgbook.com

DEDICATIONS

From Jay: To Jennifer and Matthew. You are treasures to me. Your encouragement, support and sacrifice are far more than I deserve.

From Lenny: To my wife, who embraces each of my visions (even the crazy ones) as if they were her own; to my Mom, who was the first person who told me I should write a book (when I was thirteen); and to my Dad, who told me at least a thousand times (and meant it) that I can do anything I set my mind to.

From Jeremy: To my wonderful wife and best friend, Sarah, whose giving heart, work ethic and companionship inspire me to be a better husband, friend and advisor. I love you.

ACKNOWLEDGEMENTS

Alex Haley has a picture in his office of a turtle sitting atop a fencepost. "A turtle can't get to the top of a fencepost by himself," he says, "and I have to remember that I am where I am today in large part because of the help of other people." We echo those thoughts. This book has come about because of the sacrifice and investment of many people, and named or not, we deeply appreciate everyone who had a hand in making this book a reality.

In particular, we would like to thank Glenn Yeffeth and all the staff at BenBella Books. Your continual optimism, patience, encouragement and graciousness have been truly inspiring. We are incredibly blessed to have had the chance to work with you. We are also deeply thankful to our Lord, who has given us the amazing opportunity to work together and develop incredible friendships with one another.

Jay would like to thank his parents for their undying belief in him; the Starbucks staff for letting him set up a proxy office in the back corner; Tim Akers for his encouragement; Toni Lee, Judi Carpenter, Jean Chatman and Andrea Bennett for teaching him to write; and Eddie, Paul and Thomas for allowing him to withdraw from society toward the end of this project.

Lenny would like to thank Jeremy for picking up his slack, Carl Busch for being a visionary and encouraging this project and Jay for helping him see the light at the end of the tunnel.

Jeremy would like to thank first and foremost his parents, who taught him that spiritual riches would always far exceed those gathered on earth; Lenny, for his vision in their business, radio show and book, but more importantly for the years of friendship and nonstop laughs; and Jay, for his creativity, enthusiasm and willingness to see this book through to fruition.

INTRODUCTION

What you are about to read is deeply personal to us. These are not just pages we have written, but principles we live by. We have each developed our own visions of Making Work Optional. We have each taken the Vow of Material Celibacy, and know what it is like to see something we want and can afford —but make the choice not to buy it because of the vow. We have refinanced our homes, consolidated our debt and avoided burdensome car payments. We each have created and live by budgets, and have made career decisions based on financially conservative values. We created financial plans and set specific, measurable goals. Our decisions meant short-term financial sacrifice for the sake of long-term financial health and freedom.

As tedious as the process can be at times, we realize what the payoff is—personal and financial freedom. We witnessed the ultimate encouragement of this pursuit—progress. We have seen our investments grow, our expenses decline and our income rise. The principles we are suggesting work; they are principles that we successfully live out daily. As you read these words, know that we are Making Work Optional right alongside you.

Section One: Making Work Optional

What exactly does it mean to make work optional? What sets this apart from any other financial philosophy? This is no get-rich-quick gimmick—our advice is based on the commonsense principle of living beneath your means. In this first section we give you a look at the vision behind the goal. We explain the daily practices that restrict our financial freedoms and introduce you to several real life examples of people who are already engaged in the pursuit of Making Work Optional.

– CHAPTER 1 –
THE AMERICAN DREAM?

Give me your tired, your poor,
your huddled masses.

– The Statue of Liberty

S ince 1886 millions of people have sailed into New York City harbor, pulses quickening as they took in the sight of the Statue of Liberty, a long-standing symbol of American hope. The statue stands proudly at this nation's gate, an invitation to the opportunity that is the American Dream—that anyone can realize a life of financial freedom if they work hard enough, long enough and smart enough. The opportunities of American capitalism have made possible the "rags to riches" stories of immigrants who came to our country with nothing but managed to save, invest and work their way to financial independence.

This was the dream that Dan, who owned several successful restaurants in Oklahoma City, pursued—and appeared to have achieved.

When Dan stepped into our office, we were immediately impressed. He was a perfect picture of self-assurance and success. We expected him to ask for our assistance in managing his excess monthly cash flow. We assumed that since his restaurants kept him exceptionally busy, he had little time to keep up with the financial markets and wanted our expertise to manage investments beyond his business.

We were shocked to discover what was *really* going on.

As we suspected, his restaurants were generating a substantial income for him in excess of $500,000 a year. What we did not suspect was that he had sustained a lifestyle of someone making an annual salary of $650,000 for years. Several high-priced cars, a million-dollar home in Oklahoma City, a vacation home in Colorado, three or four extended trips a year with his wife and three children, and two children in Ivy League universities had led to mounting debt. While his yearly income was greater than that of the average American, he was swimming in maxed-out bank-issued lines of credit and credit card debt. He stood on the precipice of insolvency. Even a mild drop in the popularity of his restaurants could have landed him in bankruptcy court.

Dan didn't need help investing; he needed help getting out of debt! More than a year had passed since he'd slept through the night without waking up with knots in his stomach, worried about his massive debt. He did his best to hide the financial pressure from his family in an attempt to protect them from this anxiety, but they could all feel the strain he was under. Cracks were beginning to appear in what were normally healthy and vibrant relationships with his wife and children.

How could someone making so much money possibly find himself in such extreme financial difficulty? How could he possibly allow such short-sighted financial excesses to damage his family life? How could Dan have possibly ended up on the edge of financial, emotional and relational ruin?

What happened to Dan has happened to countless people: he mistook the Great American Lie for the American Dream.

That lie tells us we can have all we want, do all we want, spend all we want, consume all we want and live any way we want—that we can have it all *right now*. And if we don't have it all, there must be something wrong with us. There is intense pressure in our culture to appear immediately and consistently successful; this, coupled with the daily barrage of advertisements designed to link success with what you own, does a great job of convincing people that they need more "stuff."

Car companies tell people they need the newest luxury sedan. Cruise lines exhort you to treat yourself to the vacation you deserve. Computer companies tout the features of the newest laptop PC. A remarkable amount of effort and creativity is utilized to persuade you that happiness can be found if only you purchase a new PDA, renovate your home, buy a new bag with matching shoes, etc.—but how can you possibly enjoy those things if you're up to your eyeballs in debt?

Unless you're fortunate enough to win the lottery, it is impossible to sustain a lifestyle like the people who inhabit those commercials without being plunged into debt. Debt is the only way a 32-year-old couple supporting two children on $80,000 a year can live in the "right" neighborhood, drive a luxury sedan and an SUV, wear clothes from the best designers and take a week's vacation to the beach in the summer and a weekend trip skiing in January, while dining out two to three times a week.

To sustain this kind of lifestyle, they arm themselves with multiple credit cards, a great relationship with the lender at their bank and a careless attitude toward their financial future. It is a simple case of living beyond their means—they max out their credit cards, get a second and third mortgage and carry two car leases, which unfortunately lead to not-so-simple consequences.

The stress of debt can lead to health problems and an overall low quality of life. Many people, plagued with worry over credit card bills, find it difficult to sleep at night. They're emotionally crippled by the crushing weight of debt, and tension at home increases with the mounting bills. It's not surprising that the number one stated reason for divorce in the United States is financial difficulty.

Of course there are many people who consider themselves more or less debt-free. Perhaps they have a mortgage, and maybe a car loan, but they've managed to avoid second mortgages and massive credit card debt. They spend their income as it comes in and hold off on paying bills until their paycheck clears. They may have relatively low debt, but they are living hand-to-mouth, saving little if anything, and doing nothing to prepare for their financial future.

Unfortunately, this hand-to-mouth existence is almost as much of a trap as a debt-ridden lifestyle. People who live hand to mouth can't change careers, go back to school, start a business or have a spouse home with the children. Despite their lack of debt, these folks are trapped by their financial lifestyle–their choices are limited. Just one major change–the onset of illness or temporary unemployment–could tip the precarious balance and plunge them into debt.

There are millions of people living this nightmare right now. But there is a way to wake up and destroy its grip, to mitigate the force of these financial and emotional consequences.

What would happen if people started seeing through the lie? What if they started pursuing freedom rather than status and "stuff"? What if they understood that pursuing a certain kind of lifestyle with no thought of the financial, mental and emotional consequences is absurdly misguided? What if they engaged in the life-changing pursuit of financial freedom that we call Making Work Optional?

What we're talking about is a financial state of being in which your assets generate enough income to replace the income from your work—so you have the choice of whether or not to work at all. This means arranging your life in such a way that work becomes *voluntary*, not necessary. Imagine working not because you have to, but because you want to. Consider for a moment what it would be like to find financial self-reliance and independence, to make your money work for you rather than working for your money. Imagine setting up your finances in such a way that you have the choice to work in the exact profession or business you want, regardless of how much it pays.

We're not suggesting that you never enjoy your savings and investments. This is certainly not freedom! The Depression generation has done a wonderful job of staying out of debt, but many of them are too afraid to actually use the wealth they have accumulated in a way that brings fulfillment. Instead, many resort to hoarding wealth and never experience the true American Dream.

Many who have come after the Depression generation have seen their parents' relationship to work and money and have chosen to pursue a decidedly different direction. Gone are the notions that they will work for one employer for thirty years, then scrape by on a pension and social security. Gone is the feeling that individuals are owed lifetime employment and security by an employer. The twenty-, thirty- and forty-somethings we interact with want nothing to do with the old notion of dependence on the employer and the government. They want to take control. They are motivated, ambitious and smart about their futures. They have pondered owning their own companies someday. Many of them have been laid off, downsized or part of a business that failed. They are extremely aware of the realities of the work world, and want more freedom than their parents have experienced—without becoming trapped in the pitfall of debt.

This generation of workers pursues financial freedom, not as an end in itself, but as a pathway to a fulfilling and satisfying life. They want work to be optional so they can have control over their personal, professional and financial lives. They want freedom from the mortgage company, the credit card company, the job and the routine that drains the passion and life from so many people.

This is a pursuit that you can join. In the following pages

we lay out a plan designed to guide you in this endeavor. We detail the specific attitudes, choices and behaviors that lead to financial freedom, independence and a life in which work is truly optional.

– CHAPTER 2 –
THE TRADE-OFF BETWEEN FREEDOM AND "STUFF"

One of the very best of all earthly possessions is self-possession.

– George D. Prentice

What if everyone was given the choice between freedom and material goods, between independence and "stuff"? Would people choose freedom—the ability to make a wide variety of choices and to have a broad array of options—even if that meant being unable to accumulate significant material possessions?

Most people would say they prefer freedom over "stuff." However, most people in our country are saying the exact opposite through their day-to-day decisions. They make small, incremental choices on a daily basis that place possessions over freedom. What good is owning an $80,000 Jaguar if it makes you so strapped for cash that paying the home mortgage each month is a tremendous difficulty? Why own a $500,000 home if it means a summer vacation is not an option?

So many people are stuck in a career they hate, but feel they can't afford to leave. Or they enjoy their career, but feel ready for a change. They feel trapped by circumstances, but the reality is that their trap has been built by the decisions they have made over time. When they chose to buy the best house and the nicest car they could afford, they added more bars to their cage.

The irony is that material possessions can often make us feel more free. Whether it is buying a laptop, leasing a car or purchasing new living room furniture, a feeling of freedom is created when people make purchases. There is a sense of freedom in driving a new car—with the sunroof open, music playing and sun shining, all feels right with the world. The more trapped we are by life, the more we value these material pleasures for the temporary respite they provide; the more we indulge in these material pleasures, the more escape-proof our trap becomes.

It's critical to step back and rethink our lives, to start making a set of financial decisions that free us, rather than trap us. In essence, that's what this book is about.

Because, very quickly, the sense of freedom created by material possessions fades. We love the new car, but what happens when the first month's lease payment shows up in the mailbox? The sense of freedom is replaced with worry and stress. Month after month, time and energy must be spent to generate sufficient revenue to make the lease payment. The expense of such a purchase is not only the extra money, but time spent with family or diving into a good book.

This extends beyond large purchases like a car or home to much smaller financial decisions: lunch destinations, DVDs and

CDs, morning coffee, a new pair of running shoes, a magazine subscription, a software upgrade, a new pair of pants, a bestselling book, etc. Do purchases like these bring enjoyment? Absolutely. Do they in incremental ways diminish personal freedom? No question. Every time a purchase is made, there is a decision to spend not just money, but also time, energy and ultimately some measure of freedom to pay for that purchase. Does this mean spending money is wrong or misguided? Certainly not! But there must be an awareness that when money is spent, time, energy and freedom are also being spent.

A critically important principle is at work here: **Personal freedom is a reality only to the degree that financial freedom is a reality.** If your current income is critical in supporting a certain kind of lifestyle, your choices are limited. A career change for lesser pay becomes impossible. Starting a business becomes an incredible difficulty. Taking significant time off from work or having one spouse quit their job to stay home with the children are not options for someone whose total current income is spent maintaining their lifestyle. If you ignore the importance of financial freedom, personal freedom will never be a reality.

* * *

Take Steven and Andrea. They met in college and married while both finishing up their senior years. Right after graduation they each landed fantastic jobs as sales reps for major pharmaceutical companies. They have been in the industry for seven years now, and their successes are obvious. They are a bright, charismatic and aggressive couple, and that has translated into wonderful career opportunities. Between the two of them, they make over $230,000 a year; plus they have company cars, generous expense accounts and several opportunities a year to travel with their companies to exotic locales.

Now in their late twenties, they are seriously considering having children, and came to us to talk about the financial implications of such a decision. Our first step was to look at their monthly cash flow. How much money was coming in the door, how much was leaving, and where was it going? What became immediately obvious was that while they had significant income, they also had significant spending habits. It was not uncommon for Andrea to take a weekend shopping trip with friends and spend upwards of two or three thousand dollars in nearby Dallas. Steven loved fly fishing, and spent several thousands each year on rods, reels, clothing, nets, sunglasses and every other conceivable fly fishing accessory. These expenses were in addition to the mortgage payment on their $450,000 home, monthly homeowner's dues and payments on their boat.

All these spending habits left them with very little extra income each month. Not counting the company match for each of their 401(k) plans, Steven and Andrea were saving and investing just under 3% a month of their gross income. They came to us scratching their heads, not knowing how they could afford a baby. We had to tell them that given their current lifestyle, a new child wasn't an option. In order to have a child, their spending habits would have to change.

Steven and Andrea responded well to our advice, and we were able to take practical steps to make financial room for a new baby. We also showed them how to start saving enough to at least protect themselves in case of an emergency, as they were one economic downturn away from financial disaster.

It eventually dawned on Steven and Andrea that they were trading freedom for material possessions, and such a trade-off could not continue indefinitely. Their case was special since financial difficulty was not the catalyst that led them to this awareness. They did not have to encounter mounting bills before realizing they were not truly free. They sought help early, and were able to preempt such a disaster. As crazy as it sounds, they simply could not afford to become parents with their current lifestyle. We laid out a plan to help them make work optional, and they started to follow it immediately. They were willing to make sacrifices in the short term—to spend less, invest more and change their attitudes toward money—so they could enjoy real financial freedom . . . and have the baby they both very much desired.

Questions to Consider

1. What spending habits can you identify in your life that are causing you to limit your personal freedom?

2. What would be the financial consequences in your life if you suddenly lost your job, became ill or for some reason could not work? How would you manage to pay the bills?

3. Do you know people who choose to live below their means so they can enjoy greater freedom? What kinds of financial choices do you see these people making so they can have this freedom? Do you see any common traits among these people?

– CHAPTER 3 –

THE VISION OF MAKING WORK OPTIONAL

We must dare, and dare again,
and go on daring.

– George Jacques Danton

Behind the concept of Making Work Optional are visions of freedom, independence, control and personal and professional satisfaction. It is a vision of individuals who are free to pursue their wildest dreams. When work is optional, you can work in whatever field you want to, in whatever state you want to, on whatever day of the week you want to. This kind of freedom allows you to work from Colorado in the summers and Florida in the winters. You can devote two years of your life to the Peace Corp, or live abroad doing missionary or diplomatic work. And whether you're simply spending afternoons at the local shelter, volunteering at church or taking classes at a local university, if you're Making Work Optional you'll have more time to get involved in your community and pursue interests and hobbies you never thought possible.

This is a powerful vision of the life that can be lived when an individual moves beyond the traditional concept of success that has been created in the United States. We are asking people to stop and think about what life could be like if they no longer had to work, but worked because they wanted to, when they wanted to.

Our vision is not about piles of money, nor is it about abstaining from all of the finer (and often more enjoyable) things in life. It is a vision of abundance, not eternal sacrifice.

One of the first steps along the way is for individuals to undergo a massive paradigm shift in the way they think about money and what it can do for them. It is crucial for individuals and families to shift from wanting money so they can *have* more, to wanting money so they can *do* more.

Let us explain.

When money is used to have things, this typically involves having something else: a new monthly payment. The monthly payment generally lasts a lot longer than the pleasure gained from the item purchased.

The natural consequence of using money to have is that often there is no money left to *do*. We always underestimate the true costs of our haves. A new car almost always means a higher insurance premium, higher annual taxes and often higher fuel costs. One of our clients, Tom, neglected these facts when he bought a Toyota 4Runner three years ago. He was surprised to find that the new insurance rates and gasoline costs mean an extra $125 per month in expenses, on top of the car payment.

A bigger house means higher natural gas bills, electricity bills, water bills for the lawn, decorating expenses, accessories and furniture. This is over and above the new higher mortgage, taxes and insurance that are part of the higher monthly payment.

Let's take a look at how this works on a smaller scale. Randy purchased a set of mountain bikes last summer. He was amazed at the cost of the necessary accessories to just make it possible to ride the bikes. He bought helmets, water bottles, water bottle holders, padded shorts and a bike holder for his car. Then, when he realized how fun it would be to pull his children behind him, he indulged in a $200 trailer for his little boys. Unfortunately, the youngest still cries every time they ride and the oldest is asleep in about three minutes. This is an excellent example of how much more expensive things are than they seem to be on the surface.

If you wanted to change professions in three years, could you make it happen? Do you have anything you want to do that people think is crazy? If not, why don't you? It is time to start thinking big about life!

Come up with something "crazy" that you want to do in four years. We're going to show you how to make it possible.

– CHAPTER 4 –
CASE STUDIES IN MAKING WORK OPTIONAL

Few things are harder to put up with than the annoyance of a good example.

– Mark Twain

There is nothing in this book that involves getting rich quick. There is nothing that involves using other people's stupidity, foolishness or naiveté to take advantage of them and profit. This is not just about building multiple streams of income so people can buy more stuff, thus needing endlessly more income.

We want our readers to understand that ours is not a cookie-cutter philosophy. It is deeply sensitive to the personal dreams of each reader. It will not be the same for every reader—it is a template anyone can follow to live their life in total financial freedom.

The readers of this book will come from many different age groups. Some will be twenty-somethings just starting in their careers. Some will be mid-career professionals who are starting to look ahead to the second half of their lives. And some will be more mature workers trying to figure what to do in the final five to ten years of their careers to make sure they can spend their retirement enjoying it the way they always envisioned they would. There is material in this book that will aid individuals in each of these situations.

As financial advisors, our favorite reply when asked what value we provide to our clients is that we help people make decisions with their lives and investments that will enable them to make work optional. For most people, their initial thought is that this is unrealistic. They have questions: Can a normal individual without some huge inheritance truly decide to do other things beside work until sixty-five? Does an individual have to have a professional designation such as a doctor or lawyer to accomplish such a feat? Is there really a method out there of being your own boss purely because you chose to act with wisdom? Can money really work for me instead of visa versa? For those doubters out there, the answer is *yes*.

As financial professionals, we have the pleasure of seeing case after case of people who have made concrete decisions about where they want to go with their financial lives and who are actively Making Work Optional. We are often inspired by the sacrifices that people are willing to make and always honored when people include us in their journey. People are taking control of their lives every day. More and more people walk into our office and say they don't want to fall further into the trap of the American Lie.

We have seen numerous examples of people bucking the

trend, beating the odds and changing everything about their financial situation in as little as two years. Sometimes it takes longer; sometimes it can be done in less time. People are taking the steps right now to make work optional in fifteen years or less. The following examples illustrate how a few different individuals and couples have already put the Making Work Optional plan into action.

* * *

John and Anne were both healthcare professionals in Oklahoma City. Anne had just finished her master's degree to become a nurse practitioner. She had offers to join a local practice making very significant income. John was doing well working as a physical therapist. However, their hearts were elsewhere. John had recently been to Cambodia for a medical mission trip and felt compelled to return. He shared this desire with Anne, and found that both their hearts were leading them in the same direction. They decided to pursue a two-year journey to do medical missions in the poorest villages of Cambodia.

One of the requirements for them to be able to go was that they leave debt-free. Many people would be stalled right there because it meant John and Anne would have to sell their Jeep, their truck and their home. However, they were not slaves to their debt or their lifestyle and were able to part with their worldly possessions. Over the next two years, the e-mails we received from John and Anne were about how many lives they were touching and how rewarding their work was for them. Having truly found their passion, they're now planning to spend many years as missionaries in Cambodia. They work hard every day, but these days are filled with joy, passion and excitement.

* * *

Tim was a successful lawyer who originally wanted to be a physician. After seven years in the legal profession, he decided it was time to pursue his heart's desire and go to medical school. Tim had lived a financially prudent life during his years as an attorney. He lived in a home that was below his means and drove an old Jeep Cherokee. Because of these decisions, he had almost no debt. When he could no longer suppress his desire to go to medical school, he could actually pursue his dream because he was not handcuffed by debt to support a fast-paced lifestyle. Tim was actually able to resign one year before medical school started to stay home with his children and do extensive volunteering in the medical profession to ready himself for his future career. If he had been saddled with massive debt, there is no way this could have been an option. Tim is following his heart and will no doubt find incredible satisfaction in being a physician.

* * *

Ron was a late thirty-something professional who had consulted for some of the largest countries all over the world. He had lived in foreign countries where he advised Fortune 500 companies on some of the most complex business strategies in the business world. But there was something missing. Ron had a love for books and wanted to write for a living. He decided that he could no longer put off his dream, so Ron spent the next two years rearranging his finances so that he could become a full-time writer. He followed the formula that we prescribe here, eliminated his debt, shored up his savings and took some drastic steps to decrease his monthly income needs. After these two years, he was ready to take the plunge. His case is extraordinary in that he was able to pursue his dream in such a short period of time. Ron's very high income and the serious changes he made to his cars and home situation allowed him to resign from his job sooner than he had previously imagined.

* * *

We once worked with a young police officer named Daniel. Like a lot of people in their twenties with a little cash in their pocket and a new job, he got the desire to spend, and spend he did. He and his wife had taken on some student loans to get through school, which in and of itself is not a bad thing. However, along with the nearly fifteen thousand in student loans he had amassed, he had also purchased a new truck. Unfortunately, because of the heavy student loans and significant credit card debt, the loan on the truck came with an interest rate of 14%. A $15,000 truck financed for sixty months at 14% ends up costing right at $21,000 after the interest is paid. Add to this several thousand dollars in credit card debt at close to 21% interest and this young man was digging a very deep hole.

When Daniel got married, he and his wife purchased a nice middle-class home that was right at the level of what the bank would approve for them. They were now officially "maxed out." Every penny that came in the door went right back out the door, with several hundred of it a month going to interest payments.

Obviously, Daniel was not thinking that work could be optional in fifteen years.

On top of all of these other financial commitments, he and his wife were thinking about starting a family His wife was employed full time but wanted to leave the workplace to stay home with her children. Thus, they were less than a year away from going to a one-income situation. This stood to cut their income by 40%.

Fortunately for Daniel, his military reserves troop was called into service on an overseas mission. This meant that he would be receiving a significant pay raise for at least a year. He would also receive pay for several months from his full-time employer while he was overseas. His wife also took on a side business and made some extra money that they planned to put toward their debt.

After speaking with us through our radio show and one-on-one meetings, Daniel made a commitment to his family. He decided to work to relieve his family of debt and other liabilities as fast as possible and start accumulating assets for his family's future. He had an excellent opportunity to use his extra income from his deployment to begin paying off his debt. He and his wife began sending every extra penny to their debt holders. Their debt load began to decrease, and their momentum increased dramatically. The light at the end of the tunnel was getting brighter and brighter. Their credit card debt was now gone, and their student loans would soon be next. A month after he and his wife found out they were pregnant, his student loans were paid in full.

Next came the biggest move of them all. They decided they could not afford their home when the baby came and his wife stopped working. He found a "fixer-upper" close to his police station and put their house up for sale. Within a week, the house was sold for a nice profit. They paid off the remaining balance on their truck and kept some of the profit to fix up their new investment. With almost no debt other than their home, they were able to quickly save enough money for a down payment on a couple of properties, and they're well on their way to Making Work Optional.

* * *

We have seen many examples of people who do not have to sacrifice much to make work optional; they are the high-income earners. The people who seem to be able to make money at everything they do. If they are in sales, they win their company's sales awards. If they are executives, they keep getting promoted, and if they are physicians or lawyers, their practices are thriving. This may be you!

Unfortunately, many people we have encountered with this type of earnings capability have fallen into the familiar trap of "Keeping up with the Joneses." However, we have encountered those select few who have avoided the temptation of spending all they make and have begun building their asset foundation. In fact, we recently advised a couple in their early thirties, making a combined income of approximately $300,000 per year. Their goal was to be retired by age forty-five. They were a pleasure to work with because they realized that to accomplish such a feat, it required them to make a financial sacrifice–to live below their means. This doesn't mean they were living like paupers; they lived in the most affluent neighborhood in our city, with two new cars out front, and took several vacations per year.

What people must understand is this: they could have afforded a lot more than what they had. With all of the toys they did enjoy, they could have enjoyed much more. How much more? Well, they sent us several thousand dollars per month to invest for them. When either of them received a large bonus or commission check, they sent it to us to invest for them. They lived off of their base salaries and invested their bonuses and commissions. What a concept!

The husband called recently and asked us to let him know how much they would have to save per year to have six million in investments in fifteen years. He wanted to put this figure up on his bathroom wall to remind himself why he was making the sacrifices he was making.

They are so serious about their quest to make work optional in fifteen years or less that even when an inheritance of $30,000 came in unexpectedly, the urge to buy a second house on the lake was forgotten, and the money was put into tax-efficient investments. The concept to catch here is that even those individuals with great earning power must make spending decisions that increase wealth. Earning power alone does not dictate whether a particular individual can make work optional.

The most powerful concept that can be learned from the above-mentioned examples is that the dream can be accomplished by anyone. Remember, the thought, "If I could just make more money, I could save more," is generally a misconception. Most people will simply increase their spending commensurate with the increased income.

Remember, discipline and planning produce results. It's not easy, but the rewards are worth it.

CHAPTER 5

THE VALUE OF MONEY

Money is like an arm or a leg—
use it or lose it.

– Henry Ford

W e've all heard the story about the young man who is offered a choice between two fortunes: one million dollars today or one dollar that is doubled every day for thirty days. On day one it is one dollar, on day two it is two dollars and day three it is four dollars and so on for thirty days. At the end of the thirty days, the fortune is his. Which one should he choose? People who have not heard the story's end may say that he should take the one million dollars now and walk away. However, the individual who understands the power of the compounding dollar knows he should choose the second fortune. How much does the second fortune become? **$536,870,912!**

A popular reality television show recently awarded a beautiful young woman one million dollars for choosing money over love. What the viewers did not know was that she was actually going to be rewarded $50,000 a year for twenty years. Why would the producers give her 50K per year instead of the lump sum of one million dollars? Which one is worth more? That question should be easy to answer. Let's assume that she could earn 8% on the one million dollars over the twenty-year period. That one million dollars would be worth $4,660,957.14 in twenty years. So how much does it actually cost the producers of the television show? It actually costs them $490,907.37. That is another example of the power of the compounding dollar, otherwise known as the time value of money.

Money does not grow linearly when it is invested and left to grow. We typically think in terms of linear addition, like one plus one equals two. But that does not work when we are looking at how money grows with compounding interest. In simple terms, money grows more along the lines of one plus one equals three. Let us explain.

If someone invests $60,000 dollars and that money grows at 7% per year for ten years, the investor will have around $120,000 after the ten-year period. Remember, if it was working linearly, the investor would just earn 7% per year on their initial $60,000 investment. Since 7% of $60,000 is $4,200, the investor (thinking linearly) would only earn $42,000 after ten years. That's $4,200 a year of interest times ten years. But, as we just showed, the investor has earned $60,000 in growth over the ten year period, not just $42,000. How is that possible? Because each year, the investor is leaving his earnings in the investment to grow. So, instead of $60,000 growing at 7%, in year two, the investor hypothetically has the original $60,000 investment plus the first year's earnings of $4,200 that is also growing at 7%. It is sort of like a snowball picking up snow as it rolls down a hill. As it picks up snow, more mass comes in contact with the ground and in turn picks up more snow, eventually becoming large enough to pose a threat to anyone standing at the bottom of the hill.

We want our readers to understand this very powerful concept because it has such an enormous impact on one's ability to achieve financial and personal freedom. The most important concept to take away from this chapter is the idea that time is the investor's best friend when it comes to accumulating money. The longer an investor's money is working for them, the faster they can control their own future. In other words, the faster our readers start investing, the faster they can make work optional.

For a reader who is going to start investing now and wants to know if he is benefiting by starting now instead of later, we offer the following example. One investor begins investing at thirty years old, invests $200 per month for ten years, then stops investing. At age sixty (assuming he earns 8% per year on his investments), having invested $24,000 over those ten years, he will have a net worth of **$170,539.96**. The second investor waits, starts investing at forty years old, and invests $200 per month for twenty years (twice as long). The second investor will have invested $48,000 but by age sixty will only have a net worth of **$117,804.08**. The difference is remarkable: the first investor laid out only half the amount of the second investor, but ended up with $52,735.88 more. Time is on the side of the investor who starts now; it is up to each investor to use this incredibly powerful tool to their advantage.

How about a real life example? We worked with a physician who, by his own admission, knew absolutely nothing about investing. He did not follow his pension plan, its results or the investments that his company had him in (not that we recommend that). He had worked for thirty years at the same surgery center, the entire time putting 10% of his monthly income into his retirement plan. He never made millions of dollars, never made any brilliant investment moves and did not spend his free time obsessing over his investments. He did, however, manage to accumulate three million dollars in his retirement account. That was enough for him to live off of for the rest of his life and to leave his three children a sizeable inheritance.

The moral of the story is simple: saving early in life is worth much more than saving late in life. Unfortunately, you can't decide today to have saved ten years ago. But you can decide to save today. The best time to start is now!

CHAPTER 6

GETTING REAL

---

*Freedom is nothing else but
a chance to be better.*

– Albert Camus

The essence of Making Work Optional is a very simple idea. Live well below your means, save the difference and over time your nest egg will grow until it generates enough income to support the lifestyle you choose.

It's a simple idea, but not an easy one. There's nothing sexy or exciting about spending less; most of us are always trying to spend less and are not doing a very good job at it. The very idea of trying to spend significantly less seems depressing, if not impossible. But that's because most of us are focused on the small picture rather than the big picture.

Whether we earn $30,000 per year or $200,000 per year, for most of us, most of our income is eaten up by fixed expenses. The rent or mortgage, the car payment, utilities and debt payments. There's also a set of pseudo-fixed expenses. These aren't really fixed, but they might as well be, because these expenses are pretty much automatic. If you go out to lunch every day and never consider doing otherwise, that's a pseudo-fixed expense. If you get your hair done at a fancy salon each month, that's a pseudo-fixed expense.

What's left after your fixed expenses and your pseudo-fixed expenses is your discretionary income: the money you can spend on anything you want. For most people, discretionary income is a very small part of their total income, often as low as 2–10% of their actual income. So when most people think about reducing expenses, or saving, they are thinking about cutting into their discretionary income. And this is quite painful, as this is the money people use for the day-to-day pleasures in life. This is the small picture; from this perspective it does seem almost impossible to save a significant amount of money.

But the big picture looks very different. Let's say your goal was to save 25% of your income. This means that if you make $60,000, you have to live the lifestyle of someone who makes $45,000. If you make $150,000, you have to live the lifestyle of someone who makes $112,500.

The fact of the matter is that people from around this country earn a vast array of incomes, but whether the income level is $35,000, $100,000 or $250,000 or more, what so many people have in common is the feeling that money is tight, saving is difficult and discretionary funds are hard to come by. Regardless of income, people are right when they say that money is tight. Whatever the income level, most people have made a series of decisions over the years without consciously thinking about it that resulted in a lifestyle that consumes all the money they earn. As hard as it may seem to someone making $35,000 a year, those making over $100,000 struggle with money. Often the struggle is more intense than what the $35,000-a-year earner faces. Why is this? Because it is extremely easy to make decisions gradually that create obligations before income is even earned. It does not matter whether the car payment is $150 a month or $5,000 a month; when someone commits to a car payment, they are obligating themselves to pay for something with money they have not yet earned. The behavior is the same regardless of the income level.

To do this successfully might mean changing every aspect of your life–the house you live in, the car you drive, the luxuries you indulge in. It won't be easy. It will mean changing some habits and getting used to some differences. There will be a difficult adjustment period. It might seem too unpleasant to contemplate.

But think about the big picture. Are people who make $112,500 really less happy than people who make $150,000? Maybe you can remember when you made 25% less than you do now. Were you less happy then? You got used to spending the extra 25%, sure, but did it really make you happier?

Science is on our side here: sociologists have found no significant correlation between happiness and income. We all want more money, but somehow it isn't making us happier.

Now consider this: would you be happier knowing that you could leave your job at any time with no financial consequences? If you could decide to take a year off to travel the world? If you could take summers off to play with your children? If you could spend your life doing what rewards you, regardless of the financial implications? Most of us would agree that this would be a much more profound source of happiness than the difference between a $112,500 lifestyle and a $150,000 one.

So how much will you have to save? Obviously this depends on your situation.

1. **How long do you want to wait before work is optional?**

   Ten years? Fifteen years? Twenty years or more? The longer you are willing to wait before work becomes optional, the less aggressive you will have to be in saving and investing now.

2. **How aggressive do you want to be with your investments?**

   Some investors are comfortable with having the majority of their money in equity investments such as stocks and mutual funds. Others desire the security of bonds and CDs because of the greater degree of safety they provide. Keep in mind: the more aggressive you are with your investments, the greater return you can expect to receive. This may lead to the need for less time or less savings now. A financial planner can help you determine how aggressive you should be with your investments.

   You must also consider how old you want to be before you start shifting your investments into more conservative options. For instance, a twenty-five-year-old can afford to be invested primarily in equities. A sixty-five-year-old does not have that luxury. His investments pr-bably need to have a much higher concentration of more conservative investments such as bonds, CDs and fixed annuities.

3. **In today's dollars, how much income do you want to have when work is optional?**

   Do you need to generate enough income to completely support your current lifestyle, or do you feel comfortable assuming that you will continue to have some income (for example, half of what it is now) once work is optional?

4. **How much do you think your income will increase or decrease from year to year?**

   If you are unsure of this, it is best to be conservative. Some professions have a long history of steady earnings growth. Others are much more sporadic and unpredictable. As a general rule, it is fairly reasonable to assume your income will keep pace with general inflation.

5. **Do you anticipate any major financial events in the future?**

   Winning the lottery does not count as a valid answer to this question! Neither does the possibility of your $10,000 investment in a penny stock that your brother-in-law suggested growing to ten million. As entertaining as these might be to think about, the likelihood of their actually coming to pass is approximately zero. Examples of major financial events would include inheritances or life insurance policies of which you are the beneficiary.

Once you know the answers to these questions, you, or your

financial advisor, will need to put together a spreadsheet that looks at your income, the income you will need once you make work optional, your likely increases in income, etc., to figure out exactly what percentage of your income you will need to save in order to meet your goals.

But we can give you some general rules of thumb. Suppose you don't think your income will increase very much, you have no savings now and you expect to earn no income at all once you make work optional (pretty much the worst-case scenario). You will need to save about a third of your income to make work optional in fifteen years.

If you have some savings, expect your income to go up over time and expect to continue to earn income once work is optional, then you may only need to save 10% of your income.

It's worth pointing out that the techniques of Making Work Optional are particularly valuable to people early in their careers, whose biggest earning years are ahead of them and who haven't yet locked in the level of financial commitments that they will have in later life. It's so easy for people fresh out of school to ease into the habits of acquiring debt, living hand-to-mouth and generally living beyond their means. As each raise comes, it gets quickly eaten up by new purchases. But it doesn't have to be this way.

For people early in their careers, *Making Work Optional* can be as simple as living within your means from the start, and committing to saving a large percentage of your growth in income. Imagine starting out your career with the knowledge that you are headed for financial independence in fifteen years.

Consider Jeremy and Lisa, a couple in their late thirties who want work to be optional for both of them. In just a decade and a half, they want to be able to live at their current lifestyle without earning another dime. They currently make $60,000 a year, but since their home will be paid off in ten years and their children will be out of the house, they are comfortable with a future income of $40,000 (adjusted for inflation) to make sure their lifestyle is maintained. In the short term, increasing their income is not a realistic option, so they will have to make their goals work at their current income for the foreseeable future. They are starting out with $100,000 in current retirement and investment accounts.

They assume very conservatively that inflation will be 3.5%. They also assume that their investments will average 8% a year growth after taxes. Based on all these assumptions, their savings and investments will earn a net return of 4.5% after taxes and inflation.

If these conservative assumptions hold true, Jeremy and Lisa will have to start setting aside approximately one third of their income a year for the next fifteen years to reach their goals. Many would say this is impossible, but clearly it is not. Millions of Americans lead happy lives at two thirds of Jeremy and Lisa's income. When they first realized what it would take to reach their goal of Making Work Optional in fifteen years, they were surprised at the level of sacrifice it would take. But they quickly reminded themselves that they were buying personal and financial freedom.

They also realized their assumptions were very conservative. It is entirely possible that inflation will be much less than 3.5%. Even a half percentage drop in the inflation rate would radically affect the amount they need to save. The strong probability is that both of their incomes will rise over the next fifteen years, not stay the same. It is also highly probable that at the end of fifteen years, one or both of them will choose to do something that continues to generate income. Jeremy is currently a college professor; it's highly likely that he will continue teaching on a part-time basis. Lisa works in the marketing department of a restaurant franchise; she will likely continue doing contract work for the company even though she may not work full time. They could also choose to extend their goal to eighteen or twenty years. Should any of these possibilities come to pass, they would need even less savings and less performance from their investments.

The point, though, is that even with conservative assumptions and aggressive goals, they still have the capacity to achieve their dream of Making Work Optional. A simple visit with a financial planner or even some time spent with some financial Web sites can help anyone define specifically what is needed to make work optional in fifteen years or less.

Section Two: A Game Plan for Making Work Optional

No great task is ever achieved without a well-thought-out plan. Whether the task is winning a football game, building a house, getting an advanced degree or starting a business, a solid game plan is an indispensable component of success. The game plan serves as a guidebook to make sure its creator stays focused and on task. It creates a framework for pursuing the goal. When there is no clear game plan, people tend to wander aimlessly, get off track and distracted, and experience significant frustration and ultimate failure.

Making Work Optional is a tremendous goal. While it is well worth any cost, it is not something that can be accomplished overnight. The process takes time, and a stellar game plan makes sure that you stay focused and clear about what you are trying to accomplish.

The game plan also makes sure that progress can be mapped out and appreciated along the way. This is to make sure that the journey does not become so tedious that the goal is abandoned. A great game plan builds confidence and encouragement; this is the kind of plan that the following chapters will help you build.

The plan is simple:

Step One: Define Your Vision

Step Two: Analyze Your Situation

Step Three: Quantify Your Goals

Step Four: Implement Your Changes

This section will discuss each of these steps in turn.

CHAPTER 7

STEP ONE:
DEFINE YOUR VISION

Strong lives are motivated
by dynamic purposes.

– Kenneth Hildebrand

Sarah gave us a call mid-morning on a Monday. She had read an article in the paper the day before that described our strategies, and she wanted to meet with us. She was full of energy when we met later that week. As soon as we sat down, she started telling us her story. "I grew up with five brothers and sisters; so there never was a whole lot of money floating around. My parents pretty much lived paycheck to paycheck. They never told us when things were tight, but we could tell. Things would be tense around the house. Dad would work longer hours or get a second job for a while. None of us really ever talked much about it, but I decided when I was pretty young that I was not going to live that way when I was older.

"That translated into my going to law school so I could find a job that would actually pay me a decent amount of money. I've been a lawyer now for right at ten years. The money is good, and I'm definitely not living paycheck to paycheck. But over the last few years, I've just gotten kind of tired of practicing law."

We asked if there was anything else she wanted to do besides law. When we asked this, her eyes lit up and she quickly answered, "Definitely. Summer before last I was a part of a missions trip with my church to Peru. We helped build a school, and we provided medical and dental care for local villagers. That was a year and a half ago. I've already been back once, and I'm going again in a few months. I don't know if I want to be a missionary for the rest of my life, but I would love to be able to leave law and try it, even if it's only for a year or two to start.

"That's why I called you," she continued. "When I read about Making Work Optional in the paper, I thought, 'This is exactly what I've been working toward.' And I have. For the last year and a half, I've been saving and investing to have enough money to quit my job and not worry about money for at least a couple of years. I've made some great progress, but I'm hoping you can help me get there faster."

We were thoroughly impressed with Sarah's attitude, her outlook and the progress she had already made. She was already on the path to Making Work Optional, even if she hadn't known what to call it. What she needed was coaching to keep her on track and direct her toward the most effective path. What the story she shared with us demonstrates particularly well is the first and most important ingredient of this journey—a compelling vision.

Sarah knew she wanted to be a missionary for the next one to two years at least. She knew that would take significant financial sacrifice on her part, and she had already taken many constructive steps toward her goal. While she knew her vision of becoming a missionary was not for everybody, it was clearly what she wanted and needed to do. She was so captured by the idea that she was motivated to take the steps necessary to get there.

Do not miss this critical point: **To make work optional, you *must* have a compelling vision for the future**. This vision of a future life creates the power and energy to take the necessary steps to get there. Some of the steps are painful and require sacrifice. To take these steps with confidence, you must have a clear vision of a life where work is optional.

A clear vision provides the power to decide to save rather than spend. Such a vision creates energy when the time comes to make difficult choices. It provides a regular reminder that accumulating wealth is not an end in itself, but a means to an end. Making Work Optional is about clearing the financial hurdles that keep people from pursuing the life they have always envisioned.

What will your life look like when you don't have to work? Will you still work? Probably. Work is a gift; within all of us is an ingrained desire to create value and be productive in our world. We are strong advocates of continuing to work once work is optional. But we are equally strong advocates for working at something you love. Imagine what it would be like to do what you love without worrying about whether or not you're making enough money to pay the bills. Imagine the time you could devote to pursuing interests that would otherwise come last; imagine being able to drive your children to school every morning without having to rush to work to punch a clock.

Jason was in his early twenties and fresh out of college when we met with him. When we asked him about his family's attitude toward money while he was growing up, he shared an inspiring story. One of the things he appreciated most about his childhood was how involved his parents were throughout his athletic career. From the time he was eight years old until he graduated high school at age eighteen, through basketball, baseball and football season, his mom missed only one game. His dad missed a grand total of three games. Eleven years, hundreds of games and they collectively missed only four. How were they able to do that? For much of that time, it was because they had arranged their business in such a way that it ran without them. Their investment in their business made it such that the business produced revenue whether they were there or not. Jason was deeply impacted by his parents' attitudes toward money and the freedom they were able to enjoy.

What would it look like to be able to make that kind of time commitment to your children? How would your family be impacted if your financial life were arranged so that work was optional? Would you be present at the music recitals, games and practices? How many parents routinely miss these because of work commitments?

Maybe you have always had a goal of getting a master's degree or a PhD, but your work never allowed it in the past.

What if you could take the next two to three years to gain an advanced degree—with no financial pressure?

Or maybe there is a career you've always wanted to pursue, but that career generally doesn't pay enough to support a family. Amy works at a bank, processing loan paperwork. She sits at a cubicle in the basement of the bank, and only sees sunlight a couple of times during bank hours. But if you ask her what she would really like to do with her life, her face immediately lights up and she talks about horses. She would love to train and care for horses, but it simply isn't financially viable for her now. If work were optional, she would be working with horses full time starting tomorrow.

Adam is a vice-president for an advertising agency. He has considered devoting his marketing and leadership expertise to his church on a half-time or even full-time basis, but the pay cut is just too significant. He is taking the needed steps so that he can make his Making Work Optional vision a reality.

Remember, everyone is headed somewhere right now. Some are headed in the right direction; others are clearly heading toward years of financial pain. As the saying goes, "If you are coasting, you are either slowing down or going downhill." When people do not have a vision for their financial lives, the only satisfaction their money brings is the ability to buy stuff. Without a clear, positive goal, there is no reason to make wise decisions with money.

So many people do not have a vision of where they want their lives to go. As Lily Tomlin said, "I always said I wanted to be somebody when I grew up. I guess I should have been more specific." Without a compelling vision of what they want to do with their time, they buy all the trappings of success instead of pursuing a life worth living. Making Work Optional hinges on having a compelling vision of what life will look like when work is optional. If that vision is simply one of having lots of material possessions, there is virtually no chance that the needed sacrifices will be made to make that possible. Why? Because for most people that is not a life worth pursuing; there is more to life than acquiring material possessions. We want you to tap into a vision that transcends possessions.

What does a compelling vision look like? What components does such a vision need to have to be worthwhile? Listed below are four key components to a compelling vision. Use these with the study questions at the end of the chapter to create your own vision for life after work is optional.

1. **A specific time frame**

    Typically, a plan for Making Work Optional has a fifteen-year time horizon. For you, it may be longer or shorter. When do you want work to be optional?

2. **A measurable income**

    It is not enough to say, "I want to get to the point where I don't have to worry about money anymore." Specify how much money you will need for work to be optional. $25,000 a year? $50,000? $150,000 or more? Be specific!

3. **How you will spend your life**

    If work is optional, when the alarm clock goes off you will have no place you *have* to be. When that happens, what will you do? Is it enough to lie out by the pool and work on your tan? Or do you want something more meaningful? Our clients have wanted to spend their lives as teachers, doing pro bono legal or medical work, volunteering at a church, synagogue or nonprofit organization, or even working at a coffee shop or as a parking attendant! For all our clients, it is this idea of *how* they will spend their days once work is optional that creates the energy needed for the hard decisions that are bound to come.

4. **Who You Will Spend Your Life With**

   In most of our conversations with clients, relationships come to the surface. The desire to make work optional is rarely a self-absorbed pursuit. It is pursued in part to be able to spend more time with key relationships—children, a spouse, parents and close friends.

We asked a number of clients, colleagues and friends to share their vision for Making Work Optional with us.

Randy wrote to us and said, "There are several passions in my life that I will pour myself into when work is optional. These are passions that I currently devote my life to, but when work is optional, the amount of time I devote to each will change greatly.

"My faith is of great importance to me. I actually spent almost five years as a pastor, and there are parts of that career I really miss. There will be a day when I will be able to speak thirty to forty times a year across the country and write a book every two years on spiritual growth and transformation.

"Right beside that is my family. As a new father to a baby

boy and husband to an unbelievably wonderful woman, I love spending time with my family. When work is optional, there will be family vacations three to four times a year. Two to three months each summer will be set aside to spend with my son while he's out of school."

Andrew shared these thoughts with us: "From the time I held my first real professional job, I have been blessed with unique financial blessings time and time again. I grew up in an area where wealth was supposed to be on display at all times. We were in an oil town during an oil boom. My family, however, did not have the kind of wealth that was being flaunted at every turn during my childhood. The success I have had as a businessperson has allowed me to enjoy some of the material possessions that I longed for through my youth, adolescence and young adulthood.

"I have been able to buy investment property, a beautiful home and two nice SUVs.

"I want my children to grow up believing that work is intended to bring personal and professional satisfaction. I do not want them to grow up believing that work is intended to make us rich or simply keep food on the table. I want my children to know that their daddy goes to work to bring value to other people's lives through his knowledge, expertise and genuine concern.

"If I have tremendous financial obligations brought on by a lust for possessions, what will I be working for? I will be working for those possessions. I will be working to pay for the choices I have made. I will not be working solely for my clients and for professional satisfaction. If I have no financial commitments tying me down, I can look someone in the eyes and tell them that the advice I am giving them is coming 100% from my heart, not from my need for money. I never want to sit across my desk from someone and view him or her as my next car payment or mortgage payment.

"I want to be free to think big, and dream big about my life and my family's life. This is what Making Work Optional is about to me. It is about being a hero to my children and a respectable man to my wife."

Now what about you? What will life look like when work is optional? In the final section of this chapter are exercises to help you craft your personal vision.

They can help you craft a vision that will provide you with the emotional, mental and spiritual fuel necessary to make work optional.

Questions to Consider: Discover Your Vision

1. If money were not a factor, what would a typical day look like for you?

2. What kinds of pursuits have you always wanted to engage in, but you have not had the time or financial resources to try?

3. Imagine that work is now optional for you. Describe how you spend your work week now that you don't have to work.

4. Imagine your life five years from now. With as much detail as possible, describe the life you are living. Where are you in your career? What does your family look like? What neighborhood do you live in? What has changed between now and then?

5. Repeat this exercise for ten years from now. Then fifteen years from now. This fifteen-year vision is what your life should look like once work is completely optional.

– CHAPTER 8 –
STEP TWO: ANALYZE YOUR SITUATION

Think like a man of action;
act like a man of thought.

– Henri Bergson

After you have established your vision it is time to determine where you are today in relation to your goal. The first step is getting honest with yourself about where you are financially; figure out exactly how you are spending your money. Most people don't know. We have had countless people come into our offices who absolutely no idea where their income is going.

One couple we advised, Shawn and Erin, had reached the end of their rope. Not only were they spending all of the money Shawn was making each month, they were also consistently draining the money Erin's parents had given her over the years in a trust account. They had no idea where all the money was going and no idea how to stop the bleeding. It was time for them to do some serious financial soul searching and analyze what was really happening. We walked them through the following exercises and helped them set up an envelope budget system (see page 103). Within a couple of months, they were making significant progress and felt much happier about their financial future.

In order to move forward, you must first go backward. Go back through six months of your financial life and see what has really been going on. Take a Saturday afternoon to study some personal history. Get out all the bank statements, cancelled checks, credit card statements: every financial record you have.

Next, make a minor financial outlay that will reap huge benefits and purchase a financial software program like Quicken or Microsoft Money. Use it to develop a Personal Profit & Loss Statement for the last six months. Use all of the expense categories we list in the zero-based budget chapter. If you do not want to buy a software program or seriously cannot afford one, make a spreadsheet with a computer or by hand.

If you have any annual expenses, make sure to put one half of the annual amount into your P&L. Semi-annual expenses should not be overlooked either. For example, many people pay their car insurance every six months. Remember to include this when drawing up your P&L Statement.

The Personal Profit & Loss Statement should look something like this:

Discretionary Expenses		
Dining Out	$	800
Entertainment	$	700
Groceries	$	3,000
Books & CDs	$	500
Total Discretionary	$	5,000
Unknown	$	7,000
Total Spending	$	33,730
Savings/Increase in Debt	$	(3,730)

Note that, in the example above, the family earned $30,000 in the six-month period and spent $33,730, resulting in an increase in their debt (or reduction in their savings) of $3,730. Despite going through six months of credit card and checking account statements, $7,000 of their spending is unknown, mostly due to cash expenditures.

After you have come to grips with the reality of your financial past, it is time to move forward. For the next thirty days, track your actual spending to the dollar. Get receipts for everything, or take notes. This will help you understand exactly what you are spending your money on. It will also allow you to develop a one-month P&L that shows how you are really spending your money. Successful businesses must do this every month. You are your own business! Remember to include coffee shop receipts, gas station treats, fast food expenses, everything. You will probably be surprised at what you find.

One couple we helped, Ryan and Nonna, was amazed. When they went back and analyzed their expenses, they found they were spending close to $500 every month eating out with their children. The casual dining industry on their side of town was booming thanks to them. Once they identified this massive expense, they made some drastic changes in their dining habits and redirected the savings. They began putting $150 a month into each daughter's college account and another $100 per month away for each daughter's wedding. Their nightly dining adventures will now translate into tens of thousands of dollars for their daughters' college educations and dream weddings. Knowing where your money is going is the first step to being able to decide where it should go.

Finally, divide your spending between fixed and discretionary spending. Fixed spending includes monthly bills like mortgages and car payments. Discretionary spending includes things that can be adjusted like groceries, entertainment, etc. The percentage of discretionary spending tells you a lot. If you have a large amount of discretionary spending, then small changes can be made in spending habits that can help increase your savings dramatically. In this case, changes to things like houses and cars can often be avoided. However, if you have only a very small amount of discretionary spending compared to fixed expenses, savings can be harder to come by. In this case, savings often have to come by making major life changes, like the ones we address in chapter 12. If the thought of making major changes in your lifestyle scares you, remember this: most people feel richer when they have more discretionary income to spend and save. Having expensive items that require high fixed expenses often make people feel poorer instead of richer.

We worked with a retired Air Force officer who at the time worked for a major company in Tulsa. He and his wife were a perfect example of a couple who kept their fixed expenses low and felt richer because of it. If there was a big Oklahoma University (OU) football game that everyone wanted to attend, we could bank on it that they would be there. When OU went to the National Championship game in 2000, they were there. When OU went to the Rose Bowl in 2002, they were there. Did this couple make $200,000 to 300,000 per year? No, they made a combined $90,000 per year. In addition to being able to indulge in these cross-country football adventures, they religiously saved 15% of their income month after month. They kept their fixed expenses low and were able to keep their enjoyment of their income very high.

Discover Where Your Money is Going

1. Dig out all financial history for the last six months.

2. Create a P&L Statement for the last six months.

3. Track your expenses to the dollar for one month.

4. Identify your fixed/discretionary expense ratio.

CHAPTER 9

STEP THREE:
QUANTIFY YOUR GOALS

Mathematics may be defined as the subject in which we never know what we are talking about, nor whether what we are saying is true.

– Bertrand Russell

Amanda called us after listening to our radio show for several weeks. She had invested a substantial amount of time and energy writing out a very specific vision for her life, and told us she was excited about that vision and deeply wanted it to become reality. But she felt like she was at an impasse and really did not know what steps to take next to actualize her vision.

We invited her to sit down with us and review her current situation. As we talked with Amanda, it was quickly apparent that a significant gap existed between where she currently was financially and where she wanted to be in the next fifteen years. She was working as a reporter at a local independent paper, so her income was fairly low. She was only three years removed from college, so student loans were still a sizeable monthly expense for her. Amanda was really struggling with understanding how she could go from having to work to pay the rent each month to working because she wanted to and because she enjoyed her profession. She did not know where to start.

Amanda's problem is a common one. You know where you are, where you want to be. But there appears to be a huge disparity between those two places, and no clear-cut way to bridge the gap. If that is the case, what do you do? How can that chasm be crossed?

The key is to quantify your goals. Remember the old question, "How do you eat an elephant?" The answer is, "One bite at a time." Spend some time defining the smaller goals you need to meet in order to move from where you are to where you want to be.

With that said, let us turn our attention to a three-step process to quantifying your goals.

1. Determine your savings goal

You've determined your vision for Making Work Optional. You've decided how much your investments will need to earn once work becomes optional. You've decided how long you want it to be before you get there. Now it's time to figure out exactly how much you need to save to achieve your goal.

Let's say you are a lawyer currently making $100,000 annually. Your goal is to have investments that generate $50,000 per year in fifteen years. You currently have no savings, and you assume that your income will grow at 5% per year and your investments will grow at 6% per year, after tax. In this scenario, you need to save 25% of your income each year to achieve your goal.

You can do this calculation for your own situation in one of three ways:

1) If you are good with Excel, it's fairly easy to develop a spreadsheet that tracks all of your assumptions and calculates how much you need to save.

2) There are a number of financial planning tools or Web sites that can help you make this calculation.

3) Meet with an investment advisor who can easily calculate this for you.

2. **Develop a "zero-based" budget**

You've determined your savings goal, so you know the total amount you need to reduce your spending by. This probably looks like a pretty big number, perhaps an impossible one. So don't start by trying to squeeze your current spending into a smaller budget—it won't fit!

Instead, create a zero-based budget. Suppose you determine that you have to save 25% of your income. Imagine that you just moved into your city, with no possessions, no house and no car. Imagine also that your income is 25% lower. Now, design your ideal budget. Lay out how much you can afford for housing, car, insurance, clothing, etc. (If you have trouble deciding, there are numerous financial planning Web sites and books that can suggest percentages of income best spent on housing and other budget items.)

Divorcing yourself from your current possessions will

demonstrate that it's quite possible to live at this lower income—after all, millions of people already do! The only things getting in your way are your own possessions and obligations.

3. **Reconcile your ideal budget to your current expenditures**

Line up your ideal budget against your current spending. Odds are that you are spending more than you want to in almost every category.

This is where you have to face up to what truly needs to happen for you to make work optional. You need to go though budget item by budget item and determine how to get this item to your ideal budget level. If you can't, then another budget item has to be cut even more.

This is a challenging process, no doubt, and you and your spouse should work on it together. You may conclude that you need to move to a less expensive home; while this is a difficult decision, it is a one-time move that will save you money every month for years to come. And keep in mind that your other house expenses are likely to go down as well.

Very often, our sense of status makes it hard for us to move down to a less expensive house. What will our friends think? Will we be seen as a failure? These emotions are the same ones that continually push us to spend all of our income on material possessions, forfeiting our freedom in the process. Have the strength to resist the urge, to resist these emotions. Think what you friends will say when you tell them you've decided to spend six months each year in Hawaii!

Alternatively, you may decide to move to an equally expensive house in an excellent school system and move your children into the public schools. You may decide to trade in your luxury car for a less expensive vehicle.

Increasing your income is also an option in developing a new budget. If you have an opportunity to work over-time or do some consulting for extra income (beyond the income growth you forecast initially), this will certainly help. But keep in mind that Making Work Optional is a marathon, not a sprint. You need to develop a budget and a lifestyle that you will be comfortable with over years, not just weeks or months.

The key is to be creative and flexible and have no sacred cows. Everything is on the table; every budget item must be reconsidered. At the end of this process you need to come up with a new budget that reflects your savings goals and a list of action steps (i.e. sell the boat, trade in the car) that you need to take to make this budget work.

– CHAPTER 10–
STEP FOUR:
IMPLEMENT YOUR CHANGES

Whatever you can do or dream you can do,
begin it. Boldness has genius, power,
and magic in it. Begin it now.

– Goethe

We now move to the fourth and final step in setting up your pursuit of Making Work Optional. This chapter guides you in the specific implementation of the changes you have decided to make. It is not enough to know what you *should* do. The next step—action—must be taken as well. Let us take a look at how to begin by implementing your changes. To do this, we'll introduce the Ten Commandments of Implementation. These will help you move from idea to action and from goal to reality.

The Ten Commandments of Implementation

1. **Do something now.**

    It is far better to create an average Making Work Optional plan and actually implement the steps than it is to create the best plan in the world and never do anything with it. Achievement in any area of life, be it financial or otherwise, is at the mercy of action. No matter how wonderful your intentions, no matter how creative your ideas, if you fail to act, they're worthless. Start now.

2. **Take the vow of material celibacy**

We are not calling for lifelong material deprivation. We are calling for a Vow of Material Celibacy that ranges from one to four years in length. If you have no assets, heavy debt and limited income growth potential, your vow may need to be four or five years. If you have low consumer debt and have started accumulating some limited assets, then you may only need a one-year vow.

When you determine the particulars of your vow, it will go something like this:

1) List all of the material pleasures in which you currently indulge. BE HONEST! The lawn crew is not a necessity!

2) Calculate how much money it will free up per month if you abstain from them.

3) List all of the major purchases that can be abstained from during the length of the vow. This could mean not upgrading the car, house, boat, watch, hairstyle, Botox plan, etc.

4) Declare a moratorium on spending for this list of pleasures and purchases for the duration of the vow. (No, coming up with new material pleasures to spend on is not okay.)

5) Decide how long the vow will need to last.

6) Sign the contract and begin the vow.

3. **Start with the steps that are easiest for you**

Your plan will likely have a number of different components. In deciding which ones to start first, choose those that will come most naturally for you. Some things will be easier to deal with than others. For some it may be getting rid of their lawn service. For others it may be trading in a vehicle for one that gets better gas mileage. For still others it may be switching to generic products when they visit the grocery store. Regardless of what the steps, regardless of their size, start with steps that feel comfortable for you.

Why? So that you can create energy and momentum and progress without a great deal of sacrifice. When you see your progress, you will be motivated to take more substantial steps.

4. **Protect yourself**

As you begin to implement your changes, you are bound to have moments of weakness—moments where overspending and failing to save seems much more attractive than continuing your discipline. These experiences will invariably occur. The key is not to try to avoid them; it is to build in safeguards to protect yourself when these moments inevitably occur. The idea is to create an environment where giving in to temptation is increasingly more difficult.

For instance, give explicit instructions to your creditors that under no circumstances should you be given additional credit. Call your credit card company and tell them you do not want your maximum credit limit raised again—ever! As you pay down a card, call periodically to ask the company to lower your credit limit. This takes the option of overspending away from you; it is no longer a choice you can make.

Along with this, review your mail while standing over a trash can. If a credit card application, mail order catalog or department store sale flyer sneaks into your mail for the day, toss it in the trash can immediately. Do not give yourself the option of even considering applying, ordering or stopping by the store "just to look."

5. **Focus on the steps that have the most impact**

Canceling cable may save you forty dollars a month. Refinancing your home may save you $300 a month. Which one do you think has the most impact? If you attack the majors early in the process, you create significant momentum and progress immediately.

This tactic is not unlike that of a professional football team with a high-powered offense. Often teams with strong offenses will try for big plays early in the game. When these plays succeed, it creates confidence for them, and it creates doubt in the minds of their opponents. Go for the big play early in the game to give a tremendous boost to your confidence.

6. **Write out your plan and goals**

At the beginning of each year, we spend time reflecting on the previous year's accomplishments and challenges. We think through the key decisions and events that shaped the year and evaluate their outcomes. We then turn our attention to the coming year. We think through events that are likely to occur, decisions we will have to face and goals we want to accomplish. We take time to write out specific goals. Note that we do not just *think* about what we would like to accomplish in the next year. We actually write the goals down. We write out steps to accomplish those goals. Not only do we think through the process, but we record the process in print.

Writing out goals creates a sense of reality. These are no longer simply vague ideas, but concrete plans of action. Apply this to your Making Work Optional plan. Write out your time frame, your budget and the level of income you will have when work is optional. Write out as much of your plan and goals as possible. As you do so, remember these four rules for writing great goals:

1) *Great Goals Are Specific*

   "We want to be financially independent" is not a specific goal. "We want our investments to produce $50,000 a year in income within the next fifteen years" is wonderfully specific.

2) *Great Goals Are Measurable*

   Looking back to the previous example, there is no way to measure "financially independent." What does that mean? It could mean different things to different people. It could mean different things to you depending on the day you read it. But "$50,000 a year" and "fifteen years" are both extremely measurable. You will know at the end of the year whether you have reached your goal or not.

3) *Great Goals Are Attainable*

For someone making $40,000 a year with no immediate prospects for making much more income than that, having a goal of $150,000 in income from investments in ten years is not very realistic. It may be an admirable goal, but in the end, the odds of achieving it are very slim. Goals should encourage you to try your hardest, but they should ultimately be attainable.

4) *Great Goals Are Energizing*

For many people the idea of having investments generate $50,000 a year in income may be exciting at first glance, but the excitement generated from a goal that is purely numerical may wear off eventually. As you write out your goals, include the specifics of what that money will accomplish—family vacations, the freedom to work twenty hours a week instead of forty or fifty, the ability to give more money to a favorite charity or church. These details create energy that will sustain your enthusiasm.

7. **Display your plan and goals prominently**

While writing out goals is a major step forward, you also need to display these written goals in a place where you can review them regularly. Maybe that is the bathroom mirror, on a bedroom dresser, in the car or on an office desk. The ever-present reminder will prompt you to action and help you maintain focus on what you are trying to achieve.

8. **Assemble needed advisors**

There is a Jewish proverb that says, "Where there is no counsel, the people fall, but in a multitude of counselors, there is safety." One of the primary reasons we so strongly recommend using a professional financial advisor is because they have expertise that you simply do not have. They are aware of details that most people have no knowledge of. Whether the advisor is a certified financial planner or a CPA, you need someone who can help you modify your plan when necessary and who can recommend choices that will help you reach your goals more efficiently.

9. **Establish accountability**

When Jessica first started working toward Making Work Optional, she was incredibly excited. We helped her map out a plan with specific steps and a clear timeline. She was so excited about the process that she found herself showing her plan to her friends and family. We met with her about six months after the plan was created, and she gave us some incredibly interesting feedback. She was so energized by the process of Making Work Optional that she started telling everyone about it. They were extremely interested and supportive. When the excitement wore off a few weeks later she realized that now she had to follow through with it. She'd told too many people to back out!

What Jessica realized is that announcing her decision to others created additional incentive to follow through on her goals. It is a good idea to choose a group of friends or family members you trust and share with them what you are trying to accomplish. You will most likely find incredible support. Announcing your decision will create an added level of motivation for you to follow through.

You might also want to designate someone who will hold you accountable for your progress. This should be someone you trust and those who will speak truthfully to you if they see you wandering from the path you have chosen. In Jessica's case, when we recommended this step to her, she immediately thought of her best friend Casey. They had been friends since high school and had been in the same sorority in college. Jessica's excitement was so infectious that Casey decided to pursue *Making Work Optional* as well.

Together the two of them promised to hold each other accountable to their written plans. This meant they supported each other when tough, sacrificial decisions needed to be made. They encouraged each other with creative ideas on how to increase income and control spending. They shared investment ideas with one another, and through their accountability, a real sense of teamwork evolved.

10. **Create progress reports**

The key to following through with any great plan is regularly assessing your progress. At least once a year, you should review your budget, your goals and every other facet of your plan. The review should include the following questions:

- Which areas have shown the greatest strength and progress?
- Which areas have shown the least progress?
- What steps can I take to improve on the areas of weakness?
- What specific progress have I made toward my goals?
- What life events have occurred that will impact my ability to carry out this plan?
- Are there any adjustments that need to be made to my goals, budget and overall plan?
- What additional advisors do I need to involve in my plan?

This progress report can be typed out and included with your Making Work Optional plan. Following through with the yearly review will help you stay focused, address areas of concern and make sure your journey is as efficient as possible.

SECTION THREE: GUIDANCE FOR MAKING WORK OPTIONAL

By now, your game plan is in place. In the pages that follow, we provide you with specific strategies to help you carry out that game plan. These strategies are designed to revolutionize the way you view and interact with your money. If a person has fundamentally flawed ways of looking at and relating to money, the best game plan in the world will most likely fail, and fail spectacularly.

Think of a high school sophomore who passes his driver's test on the first try. As a reward, his absurdly wealthy father decides to give him a Lexus convertible for his sixteenth birthday. It just so happens that he passes his test just a week into his summer break; not only does he now have an incredibly expensive vehicle, he also has his father's permission to take a four-week, cross-country road trip. So with map in hand, he pulls out of his driveway and starts his journey.

However, there is a problem in this scenario. He is actually a terrible driver. He speeds; he can't keep the car in his lane; he is easily distracted by his surroundings; he gets queasy at the thought of having to parallel park. Yes, he passed his test, but barely. Now he's headed down the road in a brand new luxury convertible. He has a very detailed map and itinerary in place, but the odds of his completing his four-week jaunt without getting lost, causing damage to himself and others or having to call his father to bail him out of jail for driving 110 in a thirty-five-mile-an-hour zone is virtually zero.

So it is with Making Work Optional. A plan may be in place.

The necessary tools may be in your possession. But if your basic understanding about how money works is flawed, that plan and those tools will be of no value. The goal of this section is to help you change the way you think about money. The importance of strong cash flow and how to deal with debt will be covered in detail. We will even give you a list of ninety-nine specific ways you can practice the Vow of Material Celibacy. We will also spend some time examining career issues. If you've been feeling like you need a change, our advice on how to find a career that will accelerate the pursuit of Making Work Optional will be priceless.

CHAPTER 11

THE BIG THINGS

Own your possessions;
don't let them own you.

– Anonymous

Imagine that you are observing the hospital emergency room in your home town. You are a reporter for a local newspaper, investigating a series of recent allegations of poor patient care. You have only been in the emergency room for a few short hours, but you have already noticed a disturbing trend. Patients discuss their needs with a nurse when they first come in—chest pains, high fever, dehydration, deep cuts that clearly need stitches— before being ushered back into a private room. But when the doctors enter to examine the patients, they seem unconcerned with the problem that brought the patient to the hospital. The patient needing stitches is asked by the doctor if he has had his tonsils removed. The mother of a young girl with high fever is asked, "Has she ever had any broken bones? I think I need to check for a broken leg." Patients come in with specific complaints, but the doctor is always concerned with a completely different set of problems. He or she completely ignores the need at hand, opting instead to look for problems of much lesser urgency. You certainly have a wide range of material to choose from for your exposé!

Of course the likelihood of a group of doctors actually behaving this way is virtually nil. Doctors are trained to determine the needs of patients and treat those needs in an effort to return the patients to full health. They are prepared to notice a broad range of symptoms in order to diagnose a patient accurately.

Ignoring obvious symptoms is not something a competent doctor would ever consider doing.

But in paying attention to financial health, individuals and families regularly ignore significant warning signs and choose instead to pay attention to less urgent issues. ***Put simply, most people pay attention to minor expenses and ignore the major expenses that truly determine their financial health.***

What are the major expenses for most people? Some of the biggest include:

- House Payments
- Car Payments
- Boat Payments
- Student Loans
- Credit Card Debt Service

Trying to make work optional while ignoring the impact of these expenses *simply will not work.* For most people these make up 40–60% of monthly expenses, and failing to account for their impact is like a doctor asking for a patient's immunization records when what the patient really needs is a cast for a broken leg. The records may be important, but it's the broken bone that needs immediate attention. Targeting these larger expenses is called attacking the majors, and doing so can significantly decrease the amount of time it will take you to make work optional.

Claire and Ed attended one of our seminars and asked to meet with us as soon as possible so they could get their financial life in order. We met with them a couple of days later over breakfast. They brought with them tax returns, checking account and credit card statements, and lots of ideas on how they could improve the expenses in their household. As we listened to them review their ideas, we noticed something curious. They were completely ready to do away with cable, cancel magazine subscriptions and call off their weekly lawn service, but those expenses, along with several others, only amounted to a small percentage of their monthly total. Their mortgage payment and two car payments, however, consumed over 60% of their monthly income. Astoundingly, none of their money-saving ideas involved their home or cars. Claire and Ed were confining their cost-cutting measures to only 40% of their monthly expenses. A full 60% of their expenses did not even enter into the equation for them.

We advised them that it was not reasonable to pay attention to less than half of their expenses. We strongly suggested they consider cost-saving options with their home and cars. When we shared these ideas with them, we could tell immediately that such a thought had never crossed their minds. They seemed comfortable with the idea of downsizing their lifestyle on the smaller levels, but on these more significant expenses, their initial reaction was to shy away from making tough decisions. This was new territory for them.

At first they were somewhat closed to the idea of selling their cars and buying vehicles they could purchase outright with no need for financing. They were also resistant to downsizing their home or moving to a less expensive neighborhood. That feeling of uneasiness was to be expected; they had never considered such radical action before. But the facts of the matter were clear: they stood little chance of making significant headway toward Making Work Optional if only 40% of their monthly expenses were up for discussion.

Their initial goal was to free up $200 a month in cash flow to invest in their 401(k)s and IRAs. Without attacking the majors, they'd have had to squeeze this $200 out of expenses like lawn care, maid service and entertainment expenses. In Claire and Ed's case, there happened to be enough areas like this that would let them free up $200.

But what if they moved to a new neighborhood? They could stay in the same school district; they wouldn't have to move more than three or four miles from where they currently lived. That one decision could free up $300 or more a month in cash flow. If they bought a smaller home, or picked a neighborhood with cheaper homeowner dues or bought an older home, they could immediately free up hundreds of dollars in cash flow.

Looking at it from this vantage point, Claire and Ed were much more open to the idea. We counseled them to start with the major expenses and work their way down to cutting their smaller, more discretionary expenses.

* * *

If you are still not convinced of the need to attack the majors, consider this additional fact: if you confine your cutting to your smaller monthly expenses, you will be so limited in discretionary spending that the situation will be unsustainable. For instance, how realistic is it for you to eliminate monthly entertainment expenses by 50%? Perhaps it is realistic for a few months or a year, but what about five years, or ten, or even fifteen? This requires an amazing amount of will power and a level of determination that the vast majority of people simply do not have.

Moving, as painful as it might be, is a one-time decision that will yield savings month after month. Instead of making the process more painful, attacking the majors can actually make your pursuit of Making Work Optional easier and more enjoyable.

Let's look at six ways you can Attack the Majors, starting with the easiest:

1. **Refinance your home**

   This can be an incredibly simple process, and depending on the difference between the current interest rate you are paying now and the interest rates available to you, the savings can be extraordinary. Before you assume that refinancing is out of the question, at least make a call to a mortgage company. Also keep in mind how the appreciation of your home can affect refinancing. If your home has increased substantially in value, that means you have increased equity in your home. Increased equity means lower mortgage rates.

2. **Consolidate credit card or student loan debt**

This is another incredibly easy step to take. A quick search on the Internet will likely turn up half a dozen credit card companies wanting you to transfer your current balances to their company. Transferring and consolidating balances usually means you get a rock-bottom interest rate, at least initially. The interest rate difference means you may be able to pay off the balances much more quickly since less money is going toward interest expenses and more is directed to principle payments.

The same holds for student loan debt. Check around for consolidation options. Signing a few simple forms could mean a substantial drop in your current interest rate and hundreds of dollars of savings for you.

3. **If you rent, strongly consider buying a home**

Mortgage interest is tax-deductible. For most homeowners, this is their most significant deduction each year at tax time. If you are paying $800 a month renting a house or apartment, you can make that same payment on a mortgage, and in most cases, $600 or more of that payment will be tax-deductible. If the expense is going to be there, you may as well get tax benefits from it.

But be warned: home ownership comes with expenses you may not initially be aware of. Maintenance and all utilities costs become your responsibility, and many neighborhoods have dues that all homeowners pay. So before you buy a home, consider those additional expenses you may incur. For most people, even these new expenses are more than offset by the tax savings that comes from owning your own home.

There are some neighborhoods in which rents are considerably cheaper than buying a home, and in which it may make more sense to rent. If you suspect this is true in your case, do the math, but be sure to factor in the tax savings and the equity you would be building in your home.

4. **Trade down to a less expensive car**

If you buy a new luxury sedan, chances are you are financing a large percentage of the cost. What if you bought the same make and model vehicle, but instead of buying this year's model, bought the five-year-old version? The savings would most likely be incredible. You may even be able to buy the car outright instead of financing.

5. **If you own more than one vehicle, get rid of one of them**

While it may mean paying more attention to schedules so that everyone can get where they need to go, getting rid of a vehicle is one of the most significant attacks on the majors that you can make. Imagine the savings that could come from having one less vehicle! One less car payment, one less insurance payment; less gas expense, less maintenance expenses. These savings can easily add up to hundreds of dollars each month.

This becomes a very feasible option if the people in your family take similar routes to work and school, or if you live close to where you work. Just the little advanced planning it takes to make sure no one gets left without transportation can make this a phenomenal money-saving reality.

6. **Downsize to a smaller home or a less expensive neighborhood**

This seems to be a very daring suggestion; you're probably thinking that you are running out of room as it is, or worrying what your friends will think.

Regardless of your initial reaction, consider a few things:

- Moving to a smaller house does not have to translate into feeling like you have less room. Some homes are arranged poorly, and moving into a home that is even several hundred square feet smaller can actually feel very similar if the layout is more practical.

- Moving to a less expensive neighborhood may not only mean that your cost per square foot is less, but that the neighborhood dues are likely to be less as well.

- If you explain to friends and family why you are making the change, their respect for you will likely skyrocket. You can even loan them your copy of *Making Work Optional*!

Are these drastic recommendations? They absolutely are. But decisions of this magnitude have the capacity to equally drastically accelerate the pursuit of Making Work Optional. Canceling cable television may cut forty dollars a month from your expenses, but getting rid of a car can save hundreds a month in car payments, insurance, gas and maintenance.

Attack the Majors! You will make tremendous strides very quickly, see immediate progress toward your goals and, in the end, you may discover it wasn't anywhere near as tough as you thought it was going to be.

– CHAPTER 12 –
NINETY-NINE WAYS TO LIVE THE VOW OF MATERIAL CELIBACY

Money won't buy happiness, but it will pay the salaries of a huge research staff to study the problem.

– Bill Vaughan

The Vow of Material Celibacy is one of the most powerful Making Work Optional principles. This "financial sprint" can help you make significant advances in very short periods of time. In this chapter, we give you ninety-nine ways to live out the vow. Grab a pen, look over the list and mark at least ten to fifteen of these tips to incorporate immediately.

1. Use the library instead of buying books.
2. Buy books you "have to have" from used book stores.
3. Trade tapes and books with your friends instead of buying new CDs and books.
4. Use online music services rather than buying CDs. You can purchase all the best songs from a CD for less than

one dollar each, rather than spending twelve to fifteen dollars on a CD.

5. Cancel your subscription to the local paper and read it online.

6. Cancel magazine subscriptions and read them online instead.

7. Cancel cable.

8. Eat at restaurants that don't require you to leave a tip.

9. Limit how often you dine out to twice a week or less.

10. Don't order tea, a soft drink or a beer when you go out to eat.

11. Refuse to SuperSize.

12. Order regular coffee instead of Double Espresso Decaf Mocha Lattes.

13. Many coffee shops have discount or free-refill coffee cups. Buy one of these.

14. Make out your Christmas shopping list in January, and buy sale items throughout the year.

15. Carpool.

16. Drop your lawn service.

17. When possible, buy generic.

18. Don't dare buy that new car. Buy used.

19. Trade in your car for one that gets better gas mileage.

20. Don't even think about getting a car lease.

21. Hold a garage sale so you can get rid of that monthly storage facility bill.

22. Downsize your home.

23. Refinance your mortgage.

24. Consolidate your student loans.

25. Consolidate your credit card balances.

26. Make a list before you go to the grocery store and only buy what is on the list. This keeps you from impulse buying.

27. When you shop, use coupons.

28. Plan a meatless day for cooking each week. Meat is one of the more expensive foods in your diet. Mexican, Asian or pasta recipes often feature beans, cheese, peanut butter or vegetables instead of meat.

29. Buy skim milk. Usually, the lower the fat, the less expensive the milk. Besides, it's better for you!

30. Buy in bulk for items you know you will use, such as paper towels or soap.

31. Learn to cook easy, quick and delicious meals. Eating out is a killer.

32. Plan for the use of leftovers. The typical household wastes hundreds of dollars a year just by throwing away leftovers.

33. Cook in very large batches and store dinner-size portions in the freezer. How often do you go out to eat or order in just because you are too lazy to cook? Use the microwave instead.

34. Prepare brown-bag lunches when possible, or take leftovers for lunch.

35. Shop online. Often you can receive free shipping, and sales taxes do not apply.

36. Buy fall clothes in the summer and summer clothes in the fall, when they are on sale.

37. Take children's clothing to a consignment shop where they will give you money or allow you to trade for their stock.

38. Start a swap program for children's clothing. Many children's clothes are in good shape when a child grows out of them. Exchange items you have for items you need.

39. As much as possible, avoid purchasing clothing that requires dry cleaning.

40. Learn how to maintain your car. Change oil, air filters and oil filters when recommended. Using your own labor can cut costs considerably.

41. Organize your errands to avoid unnecessary trips that drive up transportation costs.

42. Consider carrying just liability coverage on any automobile that no longer has much dollar value. The ongoing cost of collision and comprehensive coverage may not make sense given what you would be paid if you had a claim.

43. Start a child-care cooperative. Co-ops provide free child care in exchange for you taking a turn at caring for the children.

44. Make gifts rather than buy them. There are hundreds of ideas online for creative gifts you can make yourself.

45. Make long distance calls when rates are lowest.

46. Cancel call waiting.

47. Rent, share or borrow household equipment that is seldom used.

48. Learn how to refinish furniture. Refinishing takes skill

and time but is an inexpensive way to acquire attractive furniture.

49. Cut down on cleaning supplies by buying all-in-one cleaners.

50. Service your furnace yearly and change filters regularly. A furnace that is well maintained with clean filters will operate more efficiently, saving you on heating costs.

51. Do the same for your air conditioning filters.

52. Turn off air conditioning and open windows in mild weather. Install an attic or roof fan, which costs less to operate than the air conditioner.

53. Maintain your home. Make minor repairs before they become major ones that require an expensive financial outlay.

54. Close off unneeded rooms and turn off the heat or air-conditioning to those rooms not being used.

55. Contact your utility company to have an expert check the insulation in your house to make sure it is adequate. Insulate open areas, such as the attic, yourself. Proper insulation provides long-term savings on your energy bill because the furnace and air conditioner will not have to run as much.

56. Get your air conditioner and furnace serviced before their respective seasons.

57. Use window shades to block the sun in summer and drafts in winter. You will spend less on heating and cooling your home.

58. Adjust your thermostat setting in both cold and hot

weather. For every degree adjusted, you can save 1%–3% on heating and cooling costs.

59. Replace high-wattage light bulbs with lower-wattage bulbs wherever possible.

60. Turn off lights, televisions and other appliances when they are not in use.

61. Save money by washing and waxing your own car.

62. Pay bills early when creditors give a discount for early payment.

63. Check to see if you are eligible for the earned income tax credit. This federal tax credit can provide a larger tax refund or cut the amount withheld from each paycheck.

64. Consider taking up less expensive sports and hobbies than you now have.

65. Analyze your insurance coverage to make sure you are adequately insured at the lowest price. Comparison shop for a better one.

66. Don't buy insurance you don't need. If you have an adequate emergency fund, increase your deductibles. Also take advantage of better rates for nonsmokers, good students and multi-car households.

67. Stay away from malls. It's too easy to spend money on impulse when browsing at a mall.

68. Pay off your credit card in full each month.

69. For major purchases, compare prices.

70. Shop for prices online, even for lower priced purchases.

71. If you're in school, search for scholarship opportunities. Millions of dollars in scholarship money go unclaimed

every year simply because no one applies.

72. Cut back on alcohol consumption. Alcohol can be incredibly expensive.

73. Take advantage of your company's flexible spending account.

74. Quit smoking. Not only will it benefit your health, it will also make a big difference in your pocketbook.

75. Set a limit on how much per month you will spend on gifts.

76. Set a limit on entertainment expenses each month.

77. "Downsize" your health club membership to a gym that may not have the newest equipment but has everything you need.

78. Eat an energy bar for breakfast rather than visiting a fast-food drive-through.

79. Avoid in-home "parties" that sell skin care products, health care items or kitchen products. The pressure to buy at these gatherings is very high.

80. Check around for the highest interest rates on savings, checking and CDs.

81. Rent a movie rather than going to the theater.

82. Bring rented movies back on time. Late fees are killer.

83. Rent movies when they are Rent One, Get One Free.

84. If you go to the theater, don't buy concessions.

85. Go to the theater during matinee hours.

86. Haggle. You will be surprised at who will drop their rates or fees. Credit card companies, mortgage companies, airlines and more will drop their prices if you just ask!

87. Engage in "Savings Sprints." Spend one week every quarter when you spend money ONLY on the necessities. Literally.

88. Toss catalogs as soon as they arrive in the mail. They are an incredible temptation.

89. Stop pampering your pet.

90. When you go on vacation, take a set amount of cash with you. Only take one credit card for emergencies, and make sure it has a low credit limit.

91. Split a meal with your spouse, child or significant other when you go to a restaurant. Meal portions in restaurants are so large that most people never eat all they are served.

92. If you have a garden or flower beds, make your own mulch with grass clippings and compost instead of buying.

93. Plant seeds rather than full-grown plants from a nursery.

94. If you have children, find restaurants where kids eat free or at a discount.

95. Avoid prepackaged groceries. Instead of buying juice boxes, buy a gallon of juice.

96. Keep your tires aired up. This increases gas mileage for your vehicle.

97. Buy all-in-one products such as contact solution or shampoo and conditioner instead of buying them separately.

98. Do larger loads of laundry.

99. Let your hair go to its natural color. Hair coloring can cost upwards of $100 a month.

CHAPTER 13

CASH FLOW IS KING

Money is a terrible master but
an excellent servant.

–PT Barnum

Normally, individuals associate the term "cash flow" with businesses, not with their personal finances. A local pastor in our city has for many years been a major advocate of treating one's personal finances as one's own personal business. That makes sense, doesn't it? You have an inflow of money each month and an outflow of money each month. To create a profitable cash flow, a business has to make sure there is more coming in than there is going out; to keep yourself from going into debt, you have to do the same.

Successful businesses control this very carefully and have full knowledge over where their dollars are going at all times. Successful individuals monitor their money with equal diligence.

Banks and other financial institutions have instituted so many channels for their customers to access to their assets that it has become ridiculously simple to spend your money and ridiculously difficult to keep track of where that money has gone.

Does this sound familiar? You have a check card that allows you to make purchases by debiting money straight from your checking account. If you do not immediately write down the debit in your checkbook ledger, it is easily forgotten. The check card also doubles as an ATM card and allows you to hit your account for cash twenty-four hours a day, seven days a week. Again, if this is not automatically written down in your ledger, it can easily be forgotten. Most people also have a checkbook that they use to pay their monthly bills. On top of this, many utility and finance companies now prefer you to pay your bills through automatic withdrawal, saying that it will save you time and the money for the stamp. What we have found is that having all these ways to access money winds up throwing people's bookkeeping right out the window.

Let's say you go to the ATM and check your balance on Tuesday. It says you have $1000 in your account. You are pleased with this and write out checks for your bills totaling $900. What happens if you forget that there is an automatic withdrawal coming out of your account the next day for your electric bill in the amount of $200? You can throw your account balance off so fast it will make your head spin. The banks love this because when you make this kind of error and bounce a couple of checks, they charge you $20 to $25 for each check that bounces. Not to mention the debacle that may ensue if the bank does not pay the checks and the company sends them through again, charging you for a second time. And let's not forget the worst-case scenario where the company you wrote the check to has their check collection agency also charge you $25 for the check that bounced. This can be disastrous.

The ultimate enemy of Making Work Optional, however, is the credit card. We explore this problem in more detail in the chapter on debt, but for now consider credit cards in terms of what they do to your cash flow. If you are using a check card, an ATM card, checks, automatic withdrawals and tellers, you are already accessing your money through five separate sources. Throwing in a credit card or two makes keeping control over the flow of your money absolutely impossible!

You cannot have six outflows of money and expect to know where all of it is going. It is impossible! And that's only if you're single. If you include a spouse, who also has six or seven ways to access your family's assets, you may be looking at twelve to fourteen open doors letting your money out. Banks and other financial institutions love all of the confusion; it creates fees of every kind. These are fees that prevent you from hanging on to your hard-earned money, fees that slow you down on your way to Making Work Optional.

If you have bounced checks multiple times, paid late fees to credit cards or paid check charges to check collection companies, if you have ever wondered at the end of the month where all of your money has disappeared to, it is imperative that you plug the holes in your cash flow.

Think One and Done

If you are truly committed to keeping more of what you earn, you *must* start thinking "one and done." What do we mean by this? If you want to squeeze the absolute maximum investment power out of what you currently earn, you must only let money flow out of one door.

Lenny's wife Paige is notoriously susceptible to getting cold. It can be eighty-five degrees in June and she will say it is a bit chilly. So, needless to say, during the bitter Oklahoma winters she is constantly chilled to the bone. The natural gas company in our city sends Lenny a thirty-pound turkey for Christmas every year to thank him for his gas bill during the winter months. Why do we bring this up?

Picture the heat that flows out the door as soon as it is opened, like a river through a burst dam. If Paige wants to keep it warm in their house and Lenny wants to keep his heating bill in the low six-figures, they should open the door only briefly to let people in or out, and only have one door open at a time. Otherwise, heat is just going to explode out the doors. Heat flows toward the absence of heat; since it is cold outside in the winter, the heat flows out immediately in order to create equilibrium. Money works the same way. If you give your money the opportunity, it will leave you as fast as possible. Everyone else wants your money; there is a giant vacuum out there that is desperately trying to suck your money away from you.

If you leave six doors open in the wintertime, how much heat is going to flow out of your house? There is no way you will ever be able to keep your house warm if you have six doors open in the wintertime. Financially speaking, it is always wintertime for your money. Your money is always trying to sneak out the door and go where it is wanted the most.

To make work optional in the least amount of time possible, decide on one door that you will let your money flow out of, and then close the rest. The door may be cash only, checks only or check card only. If you have been able to use credit cards successfully in the past, get out your old statements and see if you bought things that, in the moment, seemed like a need but were really just a want. Chances are, you will spend more money with a "credit card only" system than you would using an alternative method. Believe us, the miles you earn from using the card will not make up for the extra spending.

If you are just not a cash person, or you travel and need more flexibility, then use only a check card. If you are on the road a lot for your profession, choose whichever way is most convenient, then only use that one method.

Once you have decided on the one door that you will let your money flow out of, you will find that your budget is much easier to follow.

Budgeting does not have to be a dirty word. It doesn't necessarily mean scrapping and saving and depriving yourself of everything you want. If you are making excellent money, you can give yourself a very generous budget. Even such a non-restrictive budget will still help you spend less money, just by giving you a clear idea of where your money is going. There is nothing fun about sitting down at the end of the month and wondering where several hundred dollars have gone. In some cases, you may be wondering where several *thousand* dollars went. Restricting your money's flow to a single outlet will make it far easier to keep track.

If this approach strikes you as simplistic, below your financial and intellectual level, still promise us one thing: that you will limit access to your money to just one or two avenues. Just use checks and a check card or use cash for daily expenses and checks to pay your monthly bills. Whichever method suits your taste, use it and eliminate all other pathways to your money. Two open doors are still better than six or seven.

Using the "one and done" principle, we fully believe that you will be able to decrease your monthly expenditures by up to 20% of your monthly income. If you make $10,000 per month after taxes, there is most likely up to $2,000 per month being spent that could instead be put toward the goal of Making Work Optional. The "one and done" strategy will do more than just allow you to keep more of what you earn; it will bring a sense of peace to your life and a sense of control to your finances.

The Envelope Budget System

The envelope budget system is a simple method for ensuring that you stay within your budget. One of the main reasons it is so effective is that it limits you to using cash.

Here's how it works: Get a stack of basic white envelopes. Label each envelope as one of the budget categories. After it has been determined how much money will be committed to each category, put the determined amount of cash into each envelope. When it is time to go to the grocery store, get money from the grocery envelope and take it to the grocery store. When an envelope runs out of money, you stop spending money in that category. It is that simple.

Often, there will be times when money runs out in an essential category. When this happens, it is acceptable to borrow from another category. If both the gasoline envelope and the gas tank are empty, it is time to borrow from another, less essential area. On the other hand, if the entertainment budget runs out, it is time to stop going out to eat or to the movies. It is not rocket science, but it works.

– CHAPTER 14 –
MAD MONEY

I'd like to live like a poor man
with lots of money.

– Pablo Picasso

"It has made our marriage so much better. My wife is just so much happier." What could have inspired a highly-paid professional to utter these words over coffee and breakfast with a couple of financial planners? Several months before, Frank and his wife Nancy decided to institute a budget for a "mad money," and the results, in their finances *and* their relationship, were astonishing.

Making Work Optional requires that you make some hard decisions. The big sacrifices—trading in your car, forgoing some dinners out, refraining from upgrading your house--can be difficult. But we've found that the number one thing that makes individuals feel poor is having no money for discretionary spending. It's critical that the Making Work Optional budget incorporate some "mad money" that can be spent on anything. This is particularly true for married couples, who otherwise can find the new budget almost intolerable.

When Frank and Nancy allowed themselves each some mad money every month, they found that a number of sources of friction in their relationship disappeared. There were no more petty disagreements about where all the money was going. There were no more hours spent arguing over whose fault it was that extra thousand dollars got away from them.

Frank shared one particularly telling story of how helpful their system had been. He and his wife gave themselves each $100 per week of mad money to use however they wanted. Nancy's parents were moving one week, so Nancy decided to buy her parents a few bags of groceries to ease the transition into their new home. Frank said that in times past, this would have caused an immediate argument. The argument would have made him feel like a heel because he was resisting doing something nice for a family member. Nancy would have ended up resenting him, and he would not have enjoyed helping. Instead, it turned into a wonderful experience for both of them. Nancy used her personal money to do something nice for her family. Frank was so inspired by his wife's act of generosity that he decided to use some of his personal money to contribute to his wife's cause. Instead of being at odds over helping her family, Frank and Nancy came together to do something good. What a difference! He felt good about helping, she felt good about helping and, in addition, she was very touched by her husband's generosity. By remembering to include a set amount of spending in their budget, Frank and Nancy turned their arguments about her family, a subject married people avoid like the Ebola virus, into an opportunity to achieve a higher level of financial and marital bliss.

CHAPTER 15

DECLARING WAR
ON DEBT

Neither a borrower nor a lender be.

– William Shakespeare

Most of us cannot even fathom what life would be like without the burden of debt. What if we didn't have a car payment? What if late payment fees to credit cards were a thing of the past? Imagine not having to worry about losing a job or a large client for fear of not being able to make next month's payment. And then imagine just what could be done with that extra income if you had no monthly obligations outside of a mortgage.

Lenny has a close friend who he refers to as his "smart neighbor." He is the type of guy who does everything right with his money. He lives below his means in his choice of house, cars and everything else he does. He and his wife are both very successful in their chosen professions. They both have car allowances for their vehicles, but instead of using those car allowances to pay for half the payment on a luxury car, they use the allowance on a more modest vehicle. They have no debt at all other than their home.

Opportunities are starting to find them. They invest in the stock market and in speculative real estate projects, and have been approached to participate in some venture capital projects. How can they participate in all of these moneymaking opportunities? Because their monthly income is not fully committed to financial obligations. They have the freedom to participate in whatever opportunities come their way.

Many readers could use this example as motivation to not get into debt. The focus of this book is not strategies to relieve our readers of financial liabilities; rather, our focus has been and always will be on the gathering and building of assets. However, for the purposes of this chapter, we are focusing on one of the most damaging forms of financial behavior, and declaring war on debt.

The type of debt we are talking about here is consumer debt. This is the kind of debt that is created when you buy things on impulse at the mall or on vacation; the home equity lines of credit used to buy swimming pools, boats and cars; the credit used to take beautiful, exotic vacations; the well-worn account at the furniture emporium or the local fine clothing store. Take your pick. There are hundreds of thousands of businesses scrambling to get people to buy their products on credit.

Poorly used debt is the single biggest killer of the dream of Making Work Optional. It burdens you, weighing you down like an anchor tied around your ankles as you frantically try to keep your head above water. We have seen time and time again people about to break loose from the chains of debt, treating their debtlessness as the freedom to make further purchases that put them right back where they started. They tie down the ankle they have just freed with a new anchor, making life even harder and surfacing even more impossible. Does this sound familiar?

We will admit, the use of debt to buy cars, boats, clothes, fancy furniture, etc., can be an exciting and exhilarating thing. However, the reality of paying for these items eventually catches up to you—you realize the extra burdens these "goodies" bring. A newer, bigger house comes with increased property taxes, increased landscaping costs and more furniture, not to mention the higher house payment and interest. A new car means higher gas and insurance costs.

We have heard the following words coming out of our clients' mouths more times than we can count: "When I make more money, I will . . . ." We tell our clients that if they did not have a mortgage payment, a second mortgage payment, a school loan payment and credit card payments, they would already be making enough money to do almost everything they want.

We believe it is possible for almost anybody with income and will power to eliminate their debt. The trick is to figure out a fast and simple strategy to do so; nobody wants to turn into an accountant just to understand the amortization tables and interest rate calculations from their current debt holders. You don't have to be an expert to get in to debt; why should you have to be an expert to get out of it?

We recommend a very simple strategy commonly referred to as the Snowball Debt Strategy. One of our clients, a newlywed named Chris, used this strategy several years ago in paying off his $23,000 debt load.

Chris was determined to eliminate his debt in two years. He listed his debts from the smallest to the largest. This started with the several hundred dollars owed to his brother-in-law. Then there was the loan to buy furniture for his duplex, a debt for a $600 suit, money owed for Chris's recent honeymoon and the cost of his new wife's expensive engagement ring. It also included credit card debt that had been accumulated eating out at Chris's favorite restaurant three nights a week.

Next, Chris wrote down the minimum payment and the balance owed for each debt. He ranked each debt by the interest rate they were paying, and rewrote the list with the debt with the highest interest rate listed first. He posted the list on the wall of the bathroom so he would be reminded of his goal on a daily basis.

He and his wife instituted the "one and done" budget system, which helped them save hundreds of dollars a month that had just been flying out the window. They began applying all of the money they were saving to the highest interest debt, their Visa debt, until it was gone. Then, they took all of the money they had been using to pay off the Visa and started applying it to the next debt on the list. They had previously been paying the minimum on this debt so they would not damage their credit, and after paying off their Visa were able to send to the next debt the minimum payment plus all of the money they had been sending to the first debt.

As Chris and his wife started to cross debts off the list, they could feel the momentum building in their favor. The "one and done" system was working, and their debt was starting to disappear.

Chris and his wife systematically eliminated their debt over the next two years. They were able to pay off their final credit card balance one week after their first son was born, their goal from the start of their debt elimination plan.

People thrive on progress and achievement. It is a tremendous thrill to see the momentum start to build. As the list of debts gets shorter and the burden gets lighter, the momentum will start to carry you, and the path to Making Work Optional will seem easier than ever.

CHAPTER 16

THE X-FACTOR

If you make money your god,
it will plague you like the devil.

– Henry Fielding

Many people we have worked with have experienced a phenomenon in which, despite consistently making more and more money, they continue to fall further and further behind in their finances. Despite how supernatural the "disappearance" of these additional earnings may seem, there is a simple explanation.

People often ask themselves, "Where is all my money going?" We have already described one way money can get away from you—having too many outlets through which your money can flow. But even those who institute the "one and done" principle can still be set back by the unexpected expenses that inevitably crop up: the X-factor. Understanding the X-factor will let you break the trend of making more and more money while going further and further into debt. Instead of going down this unfortunate road, our readers will use each raise, each bonus and each new commission to accumulate more and more assets on their way to Making Work Optional.

So what exactly do we mean when we say "the X-factor"?

One of our clients, Dave, had a revelation about this often unseen budget-killer after he moved into his current home. He had previously lived in a duplex that he owned for investment purposes. He and his wife lived in one side and rented the other side out. The total mortgage was $950 per month and the renters paid $650 of it; consequently, his out-of-pocket monthly housing expense was only $300. But when Dave and his wife had their first son, they wanted to have a home of their own.

They looked at their finances and decided they could afford a $1000 per month payment on their new home. Dave's wife was able to work two days per week as a registered nurse while staying home with the new baby the rest of the time, and was going to be paid close to double per hour what she had been paid when she worked full time. Thus, their family income was going to be close to what it was before they had their child.

The problem is this: their plan was based on the best-case scenario, one in which the hospital needs Dave's wife twice a week, never cancels on her and never eliminates the program that hired her. Dave and his wife created a budget that assumed that nothing was going to change at the hospital and nothing was going to change at Dave's work. They were also depending on Dave's mother to watch the baby boy the two days a week that his wife would be working. Talk about a multitude of unforeseen variables! They planned their budget out to the last cent. One little change in their situation and they would have to start using their savings.

This is part one of the X-factor. In a world of constantly changing pay rates, benefits plans and salary structures, is it really possible to know what the future holds for the next two or three years, let alone the next thirty years? When you are making a major financial decision, consider all of the things that could very easily change in the coming months, and make sure you are not being too optimistic about what has to stay the same for your budget to continue working.

The second part of the X-factor is the invisible extra 10–20% over the purchase price that everything you own actually costs you. If Dave's house payment costs him $1,000 per month, he should have budgeted for closer to $1,200. This way, he allows for the X-factor. By not allowing for the extra 20% in expenses, Dave left the door open for the X-factor to come in and blow his entire budget, forcing him to have to dip into his savings.

Dave experienced part two of the X-factor almost immediately after purchasing his new home. Owning a home does not just consist of a house payment. It consists of hundreds of potential expenses that are impossible to accurately foresee at the time of purchase. Refrigerators with ice makers that break and cost $300, air-conditioner fans that break and cost $500, higher utilities, lawn care costs . . . The list could go on and on and on.

This was not the only purchase that caused Dave to experience the wrath of the X-factor. When Dave and his wife were expecting their first child, they purchased a sport utility vehicle. It turned out that the car payment for the 4Runner was not the only expense associated with it. Owning this bigger car also meant higher gas expenses and higher insurance expenses. The X-factor totaled close to 20% of the monthly car payment expense.

The X-factor applies to everything you buy. Even landscaping your backyard brings the X-factor into play. If you have new flowers, you had better water them very regularly—and unless you live where there is well water, that water will cost you money. If you want the flowers you've just spent so much money on to look good, you had better buy some Miracle Grow and feed them. And new landscaping just does not look right unless the grass next to it is green, so you had better get some fertilizer and start watering.

Steve was fortunate enough to be given a "free" golden retriever by his wife's cousin. The dog quickly turned into a $500 pet. The X-factor particularly comes into play with pets: veterinarian's bills, pet food, grooming, boarding, not to mention the tendencies of young pets to destroy property.

A good rule of thumb is this: when preparing your budget, plan for 10–20% of the entire budget to be put toward to the X-factor. That means that if your monthly income is $4,000, you should assume that $400 to $800 of that is going to go toward unexpected expenses. Including an X-factor category puts you well on your way to avoiding the common pitfalls that put you deeper into debt even as your income itself actually increases.

When a family gets a raise, it is very common for them to make purchases that increase their standard of living. Whether that is a nicer car or a country club membership, this kind of purchase usually requires a new monthly payment. And the entire raise usually goes directly to that new payment—without allowing for the X-factor.

Let's look at a specific example. Let's say a family makes $4,000 per month and their monthly commitments are pretty darn close to that $4000 *before* considering the X-factor. They have likely been inching a little further into debt every month.

When the primary breadwinner receives a raise of $500 per month, it is very common for the family to commit to new bills that eat up all of that new $500. First, remember that the IRS gets close to $200 of that, which already leaves only $300 left to spend.

$$\$500 - \$200 \text{ of taxes} = \$300 \text{ left to spend}$$

Then, you can safely expect the X-factor to eat up 20% of the remaining $300, or $60.

$$\$300 \times 20\% = \$60 \text{ X-factor}$$

So how much extra income does the family *really* have to work with?

$$\$300 - \$60 \text{ X-factor} = \$240 \text{ left to spend}$$

If the family forgets the X-factor and commits the entire $300 per month to new purchases, they will continue to go further into debt.

– CHAPTER 17 –
WHAT IF YOU ARE IN THE WRONG CAREER?

---

*Blessed is he who has
found his work.*

– Thomas Carlyle

When we first met with Jeff, he let us know up front that estimating his future income with any accuracy would be difficult. This was not unusual; we have worked with numerous salespeople and business owners whose income can fluctuate dramatically from year to year—or even from month to month. Jeff was the CEO of a regional marketing firm, so we assumed that a large percentage of his income came from performance and profitability bonus. This, we thought, was the reason he was so unsure about his future income.

As he continued to explain, however, we discovered that the future of his *career* was uncertain. He had been in the CEO role for a number of years, and he was burned out, bored and ready to do something different. Jeff's concern was not with the variability of his yearly bonus, but with whether or not he would even be in the marketing industry for very long.

Jeff was extremely successful as a CEO, but as he neared his mid-forties, he found himself questioning whether or not he wanted to stay in that role. He wasn't sure he even wanted to stay in the same industry.

As we probed deeper, we found that what Jeff really wanted was to be in a smaller environment—perhaps a startup company, as opposed to the well-established one where he currently worked. He did not necessarily want to leave marketing altogether, but he definitely did not want to be CEO anymore. He wanted to work with people he respected, who had tremendous talent and energy and who would challenge him to excel.

It was obvious that Jeff had amazing talents and abilities. He understood the marketing industry and was well connected. But if he continued on his current path, he would burn out completely and likely leave the industry altogether. It was obvious that Jeff could not stay in his present position for the next fifteen years as he sought to make work optional. The thought of another fifteen *days* as CEO depressed him, much less another fifteen years.

Jeff's case is not an isolated occurrence. Many people express constant frustration and depression because of their careers; they're worn out because of their careers. Many of these workers are in jobs that pay well and don't believe there's another career option available to them that will keep them in the lifestyle to which they've grown accustomed. But the stark reality is that working at a career that frustrates and depresses you for the next fifteen years is not a workable solution. If your career is not satisfying and fulfilling, or if it does not hold promise for future advancement and increased income, it is more likely to hinder than help you in your plans to make work optional.

Anyone trying to make work optional must eventually ask this question about their current career: "Is this career helping me in my quest?" It is not necessary to have the "perfect" job, but there *are* certain *types* of careers that can accelerate the pursuit of Making Work Optional.

So what does the ideal Making Work Optional career look like? It is important to realize that there is not a list of specific careers that accelerate the Making Work Optional pursuit. The secret lies in the relationship between the career and the person. There are three factors to consider:

1. **The ideal career matches your gifts and talents**

   A great question to ask is, "What am I capable of doing better than anyone else in the world?" This is an exercise to challenge your thinking about what you are *truly exceptional* at, rather than what you are just capable of doing.

   We have the privilege of working and interacting with a multitude of talented people. Most of them would be capable of doing any number of things in any number of career fields. But this very thing can be as much a curse as a blessing. Why? Because multitalented people often have great difficulty deciding *what exactly they should do with their lives.* They *could* do a dozen different things—law, medicine, finance, teaching, sales—and be successful at any of them. But which *should* they do?

Identifying the gifts and talents that generate the greatest levels of success when they are used is a critical step in choosing the ideal career. It is actually incredibly helpful to create a list of your talents and gifts and single out those that are the strongest. Note that the process starts with identifying internal talents and gifts, not with choosing a career. Choosing the actual career is the last piece of the puzzle, not the first. Once your strongest gifts are identified, it is then possible to search for careers that allow for the fullest expression of those gifts.

2. **The ideal career matches your passions and interests**

"If money were not a factor, what kind of work would I love to do for the rest of my life?" The first question we asked focused on ability; this question addresses your passions and desires. "What do I really *want* to do?"

Imagine that Colin is a college student who is talented at math. His parents encouraged him to pursue an engineering degree. Because of his math skills, he made As in all his engineering classes, and was quite gifted at the subject. But Colin's interest really lay in the area of finance and investments. He consumed investment magazines and books and spent hours each morning in front of the television, catching up on the latest market news.

No amount of giftedness in any area can overcome disinterest or antipathy. Colin's math skills would clearly translate well in the investment world, and he would be extremely wise to turn his attention to a career there that would not only reward his giftedness, but also be aligned with his interests and desires.

3. The ideal career has strong future earning potential

Notice that financial concerns are the third and final component of the process. No matter how well a job pays, if it destroys your confidence and enthusiasm, it is not worth it. No job, no career, is worth that kind of price. But if your talents and desires can be fully aligned, then the search can begin for a career that will financially reward that alignment.

Once the previous questions have been answered, you can turn your attention toward specific careers. For most people there will be several career options that fit both their talents and their interests. So what determines which career should be pursued? It is at this point that the financial issue should be addressed. Which career will give you the best opportunity for future advancement and earnings? That is the career that you should strongly consider pursuing.

Let us turn our attention to one final question that consistently arises during this type of discussion: just how realistic is it to change careers? Is it really feasible for someone who has devoted years of their life to one role, career or industry to pull up stakes and move into another arena? But that is not the right question. The right question is, "If this person continues in their current job for the next fifteen years, will they actually be able to enjoy the journey and ultimately make work optional?" If the answer to that question is "no," then other options need to be sought out and pursued.

If you already know that you need to make a change, here are some principles to guide the process.

1. **Make a change sooner rather than later**

It is easier to change careers at age thirty than at age fifty-five; there is more time for training, more time for advancement and even more time for mistakes. If it is apparent that a change is needed, make it! There is absolutely no point in worrying over the situation *ad nauseum* when a change is obviously called for.

2. **Changing careers does not mean leaving everything behind**

Jeff did not necessarily want to leave the marketing industry, but he did want to leave his career as a CEO. He could still leverage his skills, his experience and his professional networks and contacts. Consulting, for example, meant a change in career, without forcing him to leave his life in marketing behind.

After spending years in an industry or at a particular job, you will have developed certain skills that can be leveraged in a future career. Such skills are portable, and any career decision should be made with at least some consideration for how experiences and skills gained from the previous career could be beneficial to the new one.

3. You can start with baby steps

For some, it simply may not be practical to change careers immediately. In many cases, it would be irresponsible to do so.

Rob deeply wants to move out of his career in pharmaceutical sales. For years he has had his heart set on film production, and he spends a great deal of time trying to figure out a way to leave his sales job and enter the film industry. The problem for Rob is threefold. First, making a change would involve a substantial pay cut, at least in the short-term. The long-term prospects are quite good, but he would need to prepare for at least a three to five year period in which he would make less than he does now. That problem is complicated by the fact that he is married and has two young children. Rob would be perfectly comfortable eating cereal and Raman noodles for the next few years; he certainly did it through college! But he is completely opposed to putting that degree of financial stress on his family.

Second, having a shot at the best opportunities in the film industry would require a move. Again, Rob would not be opposed to the idea if he were single, but moving when his daughter is preparing to enter first grade is just not an option.

Third, finding an opening in film production would likely require more experience and education than Rob currently has. He has natural ability and a strong interest in the area, but he lacks practical experience and formal training.

For Rob, it would be impractical as well as irresponsible to pack up his family, move to Los Angeles and start looking for a low-level film production job. The obstacles are too significant at this point for him to make such a decision. But that does not put career change completely out of reach.

Rob's local community college has a two-year program in film production taught by some of most respected names in the industry. Rob elected to enroll in the program, knowing it would open significant doors for him. He received high-quality training and was able to network with some of the top talent in the film industry. Rob also called around to several local production companies and asked about internship possibilities. Even with a family, Rob was able to carve out five to ten hours a week to intern with a local company. While he was not paid for the work, he received much-needed experience that will be extremely beneficial when he finishes his academic training. It is even a possibility that a full-time job will open in the city by the time the two-year program is finished, meaning that he would not even have to move.

Rob understood and acted on the fact that changing careers does not have to be an all-or-nothing enterprise. He made realistic, responsible choices that put him on a trajectory toward a new career, even though he will not fully realize his goal for another couple of years.

The choices people make in life impact their options in the future. Financial and familial responsibilities do not mean that career changes are off-limits, but may mean in some instances that smaller steps have to be taken before a larger change can be made. Baby steps are perfectly acceptable. The important thing is that you are on your way.

CHAPTER 18

IT'S A LIFESTYLE,
NOT A PROGRAM

Eat, drink and be merry,
for tomorrow ye diet.

–Lewis C. Henry

Everyone knows what it is like to start a diet. Hundreds of diet books are published each year, every one with the same message: "This diet *really* works! You may have tried diets in the past that failed, but this one is *different!*" And every year, people fall for it. They give the new diet a try only to end that diet, frustrated that it did not deliver all that it promised. A few months later they feel even more disillusioned, when even the few pounds they did lose have been gained back.

Why is that? Why do millions of Americans try diet after diet and rarely ever find lasting success?

The answer is: there is an incalculable difference between a program and a lifestyle. Virtually every diet plan is a program. There are prescribed menus, foods that can be eaten and foods that can't. The best tasting foods always fall into the off-limits category, but the dieter is still free to load up on all the tasteless celery and lettuce he wants. No one in his right mind would ever go on a modern-day diet with the expectation of staying on it indefinitely. Most diets are built to be short-term programs that produce considerable weight loss results over a relatively short period of time. Once the dieter has achieved his weight loss goal, he drops the diet and for the most part, returns to life as it was before the diet.

Many people also use this program mentality in their approach to finances. Kurt is a perfect example of this. An aggressive man in his mid-twenties, he had a deep desire for financial independence and was willing to make some extreme sacrifices to achieve his financial goals. In addition to his job in marketing, he worked as a salesperson at a clothing store on the weekends. At his request, he and his wife Julie lived in a 600-square-foot apartment located in a not-so-nice area of town. The living conditions were not particularly good, and Julie reminded him frequently of her desire to buy a house of their own. But the rent was only $400 a month, and they were able to save a few extra hundred dollars a month because of it. Any time Julie complained about their apartment, the hours he worked or the fact that he was never willing to spend any money on anything he did not consider a necessity, Kurt always countered with the promise that their sacrifices would only be for "a few more years." His reasoning was that even though the sacrifices were extreme, they would be worth it a few years down the road when they could stop worrying about money altogether.

While this approach to achieving financial freedom may work for a very small percentage of the population, it is completely unrealistic for most. Why? Because such an approach is unsustainable. Very few people are capable of making such extreme sacrifices for such extended periods of time. This is the crash diet equivalent to personal finance, and it rarely, if ever, works.

In Kurt and Julie's case, the day came when Julie absolutely insisted that the intense financial sacrifice come to an end. For her it had become not just a financial burden, but a burden on their relationship as well, and she wanted it to stop. Kurt wisely acquiesced.

But that's not the end of the story. In all their years of sacrifice, what Kurt never realized is that he did not actually know how to manage money. He knew how to sacrifice, and he knew how to live with financial deprivation. But he did not understand how to deal with the money he was saving in a responsible way. All he knew was how to avoid spending. When the moratorium on spending was over, Kurt and Julie were left with a fairly significant amount of savings and no idea how to handle it maturely.

What happened next involved a series of poor financial decisions that quickly drained away the wealth they had managed to accumulate. They bought a house but failed to budget for many of the extra costs associated with home ownership. They leased two vehicles, instead of buying, because they "deserved to treat themselves." The list of bad decisions was virtually endless. Kurt had built an unsustainable approach to their finances and when that approach broke down, their financial health failed as well.

Making Work Optional is a lifestyle. A lifestyle is not so much measured by the amount of time it takes to reach a goal as it is concerned with following indefinitely a set a principles that lead to freedom. It's important to note that the Making Work Optional lifestyle should not even be abandoned *when* work becomes optional. Making Work Optional is designed to be sustainable; these same ordering principles are to be lived out for one's entire life, not just a few short months. Because of this lifestyle attitude, Making Work Optional is designed to be a sustainable approach.

Six recommendations to keep in mind as you live out the Making Work Optional lifestyle:

1. **Making Work Optional starts with the heart**

   The decision to apply the principles detailed in this book must be made out of a deep desire for financial freedom. Attempting to live the lifestyle necessary to make work optional without the internal desire for financial freedom will not work. The choices that have to be made, the practices that must be adopted—these must begin with a sincere heartfelt commitment to the goal of Making Work Optional.

2. **Find reasons to celebrate**

   If you are starting the Making Work Optional journey with substantial credit card debt, you probably have five or more credit cards. When the balance is eliminated on one of those cards, that is reason for celebration! There is no reason to wait until $20,000 or more of credit card debt is paid off; make it a point to celebrate the smaller milestones along the way.

Celebrating may mean dinner out at a favorite restaurant. It may mean dropping the children off with some friends for the evening and then heading back home to curl up on the couch and watch a movie. Perhaps it means something as simple as a picnic in the park or buying a "Congratulations" card. Anything that does not break the bank but holds significance to you can be used to celebrate the victories you'll achieve along the way.

3. **Do not let setbacks end the journey**

The day came when Jonathan stared straight into the face of a thirty-six-inch flat screen plasma television and temptation grabbed him squarely around the wallet. He knew he should stay away from it, but he kept thinking, "This would look so incredible in my living room." Every rational thought disappeared and, giving into his past shopaholic tendencies, he purchased it. Was this in his budget? Not at all. Had he set aside money to buy it? Not even close. But he did it anyway.

The realization of what he had done set in even before he had made it out the front door of the electronics store. Jonathan had just taken a significant step backward, and now had a choice to make. He could abandon the whole enterprise, returning to the previous behaviors that had sent him into a downward spiral toward financial oblivion, or he could chalk up the purchase to a momentary lapse of reason and pick up where he left off.

While your setbacks will hopefully be much less significant they *will* occur. The important thing to remember is that a setback is not the same thing as failure. While a setback may prolong the eventual goal, it does not mean you need to desert the entire pursuit of Making Work Optional.

4. **Find others who share the same values as you**

There is no question that any set of values is easier to live out when done alongside those who share them. Whether the shared values are spiritual, relational, physical, career or financial, having people close by who share them can ease your journey significantly.

5. **If you have a family, make sure they are on board with you**

Making financial decisions with a solo mentality in a family setting is a recipe for spectacular disaster. This was certainly Kurt and Julie's situation. Kurt was willing to make financial decisions that Julie simply was not comfortable with. What Kurt did not realize was that this was damaging to his marriage. Julie was willing to go along with the sacrifices in the short-term, but when she realized that short-term was turning into long-term with no hope of ever ending, she decided she had had enough. By the time she told Kurt, serious friction had built up in their marriage, and it took quite a bit of time for them to work through the frustration that had developed.

So what if a spouse is not willing to adopt the principles of Making Work Optional? The important idea is to move slowly. Your husband may not be willing to down-size to a smaller home, but he may be willing to refinance your current home and invest the difference. Your wife may not be open to the idea of taking the Vow of Material Celibacy for the next year, but she may be open to creating a zero-based budget.

There are enough aspects to Making Work Optional that even an unwilling spouse or significant other should be able to find one or two that they are willing to apply. In most cases, once the unwilling partner sees the financial improvement that applying even a single principle can lead to, they are far more willing to apply the approach more fully.

6. **Lasting success means creating a sustainable lifestyle**

As was the case with Kurt and Julie, many people make short-term financial decisions that are completely unsustainable. No one could be expected to live out such decisions indefinitely. It is unreasonable for a family of four to live in a one-bedroom apartment for the next five years, but it may be very possible for that same family to live in a two-bedroom home. A businesswoman who lives forty-five minutes from her office cannot reasonably attempt to live without a car, but she can consider trading in her SUV for a used hybrid or economy sedan.

SECTION FOUR: THE MAKING WORK OPTIONAL SECRETS OF INVESTING

Now that you've plugged the hole in your monthly spending and learned how to make choices that will increase the amount of income you have to work with, it's time to talk about what to do with all that money you'll be saving. In this section, we give special attention to the investment considerations that will make or break your path to Making Work Optional. We are surrounded by thousands of different investment options: stocks, bonds, mutual funds, options, exchange traded funds, variable annuities, life insurance, real estate . . . . The list goes on and on.

Which investment choices are the right ones? Which will help you reach your goals, and which will simply cause frustration and failure? More to the point, are there certain investments that are better fitted than others for someone who is Making Work Optional?

These final chapters give you direction on the kinds of investments you should pay attention to—and the kinds you should avoid at all costs. We give you an in-depth look at the world of mutual funds since a vast majority of investors own mutual funds, if not through direct investment, then through their 401(k)s, IRAs and other retirement accounts. We look also at the impact that taxes have on your investments, a facet many people completely ignore. Pay particular attention to the last chapter: one of the wisest moves most investors can make is finding a quality advisor. We'll give you specific criteria to help you find an advisor who will serve as a tremendous ally on your quest.

CHAPTER 19

THE RIGHT MIX

The question with wealth is
what you do with it.

– John D. Rockefeller

If you follow the advice we have given you in the previous chapters, you will find yourself with the extra money necessary to begin investing toward your goals. Do you need to get an MBA to understand what to do? Not at all. Do you need to learn how to trade online to be able to grow your nest egg? Absolutely not. What you do need, however, is a good advisor and some basic guidelines for what to do with your surplus funds.

We have created some guidelines for how much money you as an investor should have in stocks versus bonds, depending on how many years you have left until you need the money from your investments. Below you'll find four categories with some general guidelines for each category.

Ten to fifteen years remaining: There is plenty of time left until you need your money, so you can be a bit aggressive. Be prepared to endure swings of 30–40% in your investments during these years. The swings will be the largest of any plan here, but the gains should be the biggest as well. If you are in this time category, we recommend a blend of 80% stocks and 20% bonds. Remember, this is your investment money, not your emergency savings money. When money is invested in the stock market, it can drop significantly in value in a very short period of time. It is imperative that the money being used for this plan is for long-term use, not for the groceries.

Six to ten years remaining: You still have an adequate amount of time until you need your money, so you can afford to endure some of the swings in the market. However, you will want to moderate the swings, which requires a more conservative investment stance. We recommend a blend closer to 60% stocks and 40% fixed income investments. This blend will absorb more of the shocks in the stock market while still leaving you in position to take advantage of the positive runs the market may make as well.

One to five years remaining: Time is a much bigger issue. The stock market can be very unforgiving to investors with time horizons of less than five years. We suggest keeping a modest portion of your investments, maybe 30%, in the stock market. The rest should be in conservative fixed income investments, such as bonds with maturities of less than five years. For the money that you put in the stock market, we recommend being very conservative; put your money in funds that are referred to as growth and income funds. These typically invest in large, well-established companies that pay dividends.

One month to one year remaining: Forget the stock

market; focus instead on preserving what you have worked so hard to build. It is time to switch to investments at the most conservative end of the spectrum. You may even consider calling your grandmother and asking her where she keeps her money. Use certificates of deposit, money market accounts and 12-month T-bills. There is no room for error here, so play it safe.

CHAPTER 20

INVESTMENT SCHOOL

*The only thing wealth does for some people
is make them worry about losing it.*

– Comte de Rivarol

This book is not intended to make you an investing guru, but it will help if you understand some general terms and concepts. We'll lay out some basics here, but if you want to learn more there are some great books out there that you can read to increase your level of expertise. Here are four particularly good ones:

THE RANDOM WALK GUIDE TO INVESTING: TEN RULES FOR FINANCIAL SUCCESS by Burton G. Malkiel

THE ONLY INVESTMENT GUIDE YOU'LL EVER NEED by Andrew Tobias

BOGLE ON MUTUAL FUNDS: NEW PERSPECTIVES FOR THE INTELLIGENT INVESTOR by John Bogle

STOCKS FOR THE LONG RUN: THE DEFINITIVE GUIDE TO FINANCIAL MARKET RETURNS AND LONG-TERM INVESTMENT STRATEGIES by Jeremy J. Siegel

Let us start by making it clear that we give absolutely zero credence to the "entertainment" investing networks. We believe that watching these channels faithfully actually *decreases* your chances for success.

One of the top reasons not to watch these channels for investing advice is the enormous number of varied and conflicting opinions that are presented. Each guest that comments on the future direction of the market has an equally compelling reason why their forecast is correct. Out of twenty guests, ten of them say the market is undervalued and will be heading up, and ten of them say the market is overvalued and will be heading down. How are the viewers supposed to decide who is right? Every single guest has impressive credentials, a successful track record and certainly *appears* to know more than you do. The problem is, there is absolutely no way to differentiate between opinions and figure out who to believe.

Watching these channels is like turning on the nightly news to see the weather, so you can decide if you need a coat or a short-sleeved shirt the next day. You wait patiently through all the teasers and hear some great stories about a burglary, a car chase and a cat that turned thirty years old today. Finally, the weather man comes on and makes a compelling case about why it is going to be thirty degrees tomorrow and how you had better bundle up. But wait—they are going to cover their bases this time and have a second weatherman come on. He has equally impressive credentials from a station across town and an equally compelling argument as to why it is going to be seventy-five degrees tomorrow and how you had better dress for spring weather. To top it off, they have a former member of the National Weather Advisory come on to give her opinion: that it is fruitless to try to predict the weather, and that you should just be prepared for anything. What should you do? You have no clue as to what the weather is going to be like or how to prepare for it.

CNBC works the same way. The difference is that if you wear a heavy coat and it's warm, you can take the coat off. If you make a major mistake because of the conflicting opinions you hear on CNBC, it could cost you your retirement.

Remember, the reporters on CNBC are not economics professors. CNBC is not Harvard Business School. It is not in the business of educating people. It is in the business of getting people to turn on the television and leave it on. If it showed economics professors teaching about security evaluation, portfolio management and financial statement analysis all day, no one would watch. CNBC is very similar to SportsCenter; it is a source of entertainment, not hard-core data. We believe that to make investment decisions you need to turn to history, *not* entertainment. Following CNBC is only going to cause you unnecessary stress. You are much better off ignoring its advice altogether and just sticking with your financial advisor. For the least amount of stress and worry, find an advisor who uses a process called the "modern portfolio theory." This theory won the Nobel Prize for Economics in 1990. The basic idea is that for whatever level of risk an investor is willing to take, there is a portfolio that will give the highest possible return. The modern portfolio theory comes out of looking at the market as a whole as opposed to looking at individual investment opportunities, and its predictions are for the long-term—short-term volatility and loss are expected, and prepared for, so there's no need to waste your time worrying.

Since we see your eyes glazing over already, let's make this more readable by relating your investments to food. That certainly helps keep Lenny and Jeremy's interest.

To a great number of investors, having four different mutual funds means that they have a diversified portfolio. We compare that to eating a taco, a burrito and an enchilada at Taco Bell and believing that you ate a well-balanced meal.

Think of the proper way of investing as eating a balanced diet. You have to have a certain amount of carbohydrates, proteins and fats. As you advance in age, you also start to require vitamins to supplement your diet. We will consider the above nutrient groups as the different classes of investments you need for a healthy financial portfolio.

Typically, one requires more carbohydrates than the other food groups; the investment equivalent is cap stocks. One needs a healthy amount of protein; its equivalent is small-/mid-cap stocks. International investments make up the fats category: though fats are good for you, you need to make sure to eat the right kinds, and even then in moderation.

As we mentioned, vitamins are sometimes required to supplement your food intake as you progress in age. Typically, a younger individual does not need vitamins because their body gets enough nutrients from a regular, well-balanced diet. This is why we designate vitamins to represent the fixed income category of investments; most investors who are in the earlier accumulation stage of wealth have less need for fixed income investments, just as younger eaters have less need to take vitamins.

A breakdown of some of the common terms

1. Large-cap: the 500 largest companies in U.S.

   *Represented by the S&P 500

   *These are your carbohydrates

2. Mid-cap: the next 800 largest companies

   *Represented by the S&P 400 Mid-Cap growth

   *Also represented by the S&P 400 Mid-Cap value

   *These are your proteins

3. Small-cap: the next 2000 largest companies

   *Represented by the Russell 2000

   *Also part of the protein group

4. International: companies outside the U.S.

   *Represented by the MSCI-EAFE Index Exchange Japan

   *This is your fat. You need some, but you also need to make sure to get the right kind.

Do you see where we are going with this? Most of us have tried one fad diet or another where you eat *only* one food group: all carbs, or all protein and fats. These kinds of diets may work temporarily, but you cannot sustain an "all one food group" diet for very long; it's just not healthy. The body needs nutrients from all of the different food groups.

Investing is no different. There was a giant craze in the nineties where people only invested in the S&P 500 index through index mutual funds. This worked for a while, but just as a diet stops working after a while, so did this investment strategy. We are not saying that the S&P 500 will never go up again, but the people who owned it exclusively suffered a large drop in their portfolios when it fell—and some of them didn't have the time to wait for it to recover.

Milk and Mountain Dew

Another element of investing that will aid you in your forays into investing is what we call "milk and Mountain Dew." The milk/Mountain Dew metaphor is a great way to explain what are generally considered conservative and aggressive investments.

Milk is considered a nourishing staple for growing bodies because of its high calcium content. It is often the backbone of children's diets.

On the other end of the spectrum is Mountain Dew. If you give a child Mountain Dew, it will give him or her a quick burst of frantic energy. If Mountain Dew is consumed at the right time and in the right quantities—say, half a cup before an exam—it can add a much-needed extra kick. However, when the energy runs out from the Mountain Dew, the drinker is likely to crash. A spike in energy is followed by an equally serious drop.

Milk and Mountain Dew represent respectively the "value" and "growth" portions of an investment portfolio. The milk portion will provide your portfolio with slow but steady growth. The Mountain Dew portion will provide larger bursts of growth that add some juice to a portfolio's positive long-term results.

The more you prefer stability and consistency, the more milk—larger, well-known companies—you should drink. The more you prefer to risk the fluctuations of the market, giving you potential for higher, faster growth, the more Mountain Dew—companies positioned to grow rapidly in the next few years–you should have.

Knowledge to impress your friends:

Milk = Value Stocks: companies that are in out-of-favor areas of the economy

- Stocks are usually priced at less than their fair value
- Profits are often paid out as dividends
- These are typically very large, well-known companies
- Companies are typically more stable
- Examples include: Kodak, Phillips, Southwestern Bell, Dupont, Caterpillar, General Motors, Proctor and Gamble

Mountain Dew = Growth Stocks: companies that are positioned to grow rapidly in the coming years

- Companies typically re-invest their profits for further growth
- Stocks can be very volatile
- Examples include: Microsoft, General Electric, Lowe's, Eli Lilly, Merck, AOL

The key is to diversify intelligently. If you are a business owner and you own two businesses, you must select them carefully. If you own a swimming pool company and a roofing company, when it rains you will not be able to do either. You will be shut down the entire time it is raining. Obviously, there will be very slow days and maybe even weeks.

However, imagine if you owned a swimming pool company and an umbrella company. During hot and sunny weather, you would be installing pools left and right. On those days, weeks or months (if you live in Seattle) when it rains, you would be selling umbrellas like crazy. No matter what the weather, you'll still be making money; your business will be much more consistent. The same principle holds for your portfolio—you want to invest so that no matter which way the market turns, your portfolio will continue to grow in a steady, consistent fashion.

Exercises To Get You Started

This chapter presents some guidelines on how to invest and explains some essential investing concepts. The following is a list of exercises to get you started on your investment plan.

1. Identify how much you have each month to invest.

2. Determine how many years you have until you will need to access your investments. (This can be done using the information in the chapter "Quantify Your Goals".)

3. Work to understand the general investment concepts we have presented.

4. Find an established financial advisor who uses the modern portfolio theory. Most certified financial planners use this methodology.

5. Plan to add to your investments monthly. Make it a bill that gets paid along with rent and utilities.

6. Stick with it!

– CHAPTER 21 –
WHAT ABOUT REAL ESTATE?

How I Made 356% In The Bear Market
(And How You Can Do Even Better...)

O ne of the most powerful ways to accumulate wealth in the United States is through the proper use of real estate investing. We have all heard examples of someone who made their fortune buying smaller properties that led to bigger properties that led to high-rise towers. We have also heard stories of people who accumulated rental property after rental property until they owned hundreds of paid-for houses that generated a steady income month after month.

This chapter is not intended to teach you how to invest in real estate. What it is intended to do is inform you about the pros and cons of investing in real estate. We also discuss several different family situations and how these family situations can impact the experience of real estate investment.

Success stories grab people's attention and make real estate investment look like a foolproof way to make money, but there is another side to the story. We are of the opinion that the people getting rich the fastest in real estate are the people who make television infomercials. These shows illustrate the riches that are possible with very little time and almost no money, but we do not know anyone who has bought one of these programs and made the kind of money that is advertised.

We are not saying these programs are fraudulent. What we are saying is that real estate is a huge commitment. Large rewards are possible, but risks just as large must be taken to get them.

One of the true powers of real estate is the power to leverage money. Leveraging money means that an investor can buy a $100,000 property with only $20,000 of their own funds; the bank's money is used for the rest. That sounds great. The problem is that people can get in over their heads if they are not well-educated in the area of real estate. Often the individual trying to get into buying properties is buying from someone who has been in real estate for a long time. Most of the time the person with experience will get the better deal, and the inexperienced investor will lose money.

Clients and friends often ask us whether we think they should get into buying properties or stick to stock market investing. The answer varies from person to person because each individual's lifestyle is so different. Let's look at some different types of family arrangements to see the impact these arrangements have on the feasibility of investing real estate.

Type 1: Single, no dependants

One of our clients told us he went all four years during college without ever having a television in his room. He had never been as productive before and has never been as productive since. He was able to achieve success academically, socially and organizationally because he was able to use every minute of every day to its fullest.

If you are single and have no one depending on you, you are in the position to make work optional more quickly because of the time and energy you can devote to the lifestyle.

If you belong to this group, you should sell your televisions, Nintendos and PlayStations and start spending your evenings looking for real estate properties, or working on a "fixer-upper".

The area of real estate investing may very well be a perfect fit for you. There are several excellent books that can help. Also consider looking for an experienced real estate investor to take you under their wing.

Type 2: Young couple, modestly successful careers, no kids

When we met Brad, he was a young professional in Oklahoma City, married with no children. His father has been very successful in using real estate investing, and Brad decided to follow in his lucrative footsteps. When Brad and his wife were looking for their first house, they decided to look for a duplex to purchase. The idea was that they would live in one half and rent out the other. They were fortunate to find one in the right area at the right price. This has been an excellent investment for Brad—he and his wife now rent out both sides, generating positive income each month. The property will be paid for in eleven years and has appreciated in value because of the location. Because it was just the two of them, Brad and his wife were well suited for this kind of investment.

Type 3: Couple, wildly successful careers, no kids

Frankly, we believe that real estate is not the best strategy for couples who fall into this category. To make the kind of money these couples make typically requires long hours at work, lots of travel and occasional work in the evenings and on weekends. The couple's time together may seem fleeting at best. We never advocate people putting Making Work Optional above their personal relationships. Thus, if you fall into the above category, we generally recommend that you use passive investments that do not require your time and energy in order for them to succeed.

Typically, we recommend that people in this situation invest in the single most powerful wealth-building tool ever created: the United States stock market. Most couples in this category should not waste their time on "fixer-uppers". It takes a tremendous time commitment to learn how to identify undervalued real estate properties, and even after these gems have been identified, it takes even more time and energy to go out and find them. Most real estate experts recommend looking at 100 properties to find one that is worth buying, and that is simply not a worthwhile use of most successful professional couples' free time.

Type 4: Young couple with children

We have worked with several couples that fall into this category. We mentioned Brad earlier. When he bought his first property, he was married but had no children. Now, he and Julie have two young boys. Brad originally aspired to purchase one or two properties per year for the next fifteen years. He wanted to build streams of income from multiple properties that would support his lifestyle for the rest of his life. But then his wife announced that she was pregnant. Everything changed! What was once a simple trip to the duplex to meet with a plumber, electrician or appliance guy became something much more complicated. Julie would have to schedule the meeting around nap and feeding times. She would often then wait at the duplex with the children in the car for forty-five minutes to an hour because people in the repair and service business tend to run late. If the repair person needed to go pick up parts, Julie and the boys would have to wait in the car until the repair person returned. If the repair person never showed up in the first place, Julie would have to head home after waiting for close to an hour and re-schedule the appointment. See what we mean? Brad could not be there because he was running his business during the same hours in which the service people were usually able to come. This was not a big deal when Julie could fly over there after her shift as a registered nurse at a hospital a mile away from the property, but children made this kind of flexibility impossible. Brad and his wife have since decided that the duplex was too much work, and recently sold it.

Investing in real estate is never as easy or as glamorous as it sounds, but it can be very profitable for the right person or family. Weigh the decision carefully, and make sure to use a professional realtor to help you get started.

CHAPTER 22

THE MUTUAL FUND EDGE

---

*[The mutual fund] industry
has lost its way. A half-century
ago, it was far more an investment
business than a marketing business.
Today, the reverse is true.*

–John Bogle

The purpose of this book is to give you a template for how to use the accumulation of assets to provide you with an income stream for life, giving you the choice of whether or not to work. But just what assets should you invest in to accomplish your goals? This chapter will answer that question.

We have already discussed some of the possibilities that may exist for you in investments such as real estate; this chapter will focus on the factors you need to be aware of when investing in mutual funds. To do so, we are going to sort our way through the plethora of available options. Remember, there is no "one size fits all" investment.

The first thing to realize is that the vast majority of people reading this book do not have the skills necessary to successfully invest in individual stocks. A mutual fund is a way for investors to both pool their money with others and have access to a professional money manager. The concept is great in theory, and for some people, these investments fit like a glove. For those just getting started in investing who want to put money away on a consistent monthly basis, there is no better tool than mutual funds.

Investing blindly in any mutual fund, however, can be a serious stumbling block on the way to Making Work Optional. All funds are not created equal. During the boom in funds during the last decade, there have been many funds that are just not worthy of your money. We are not trying to say they are bad investments—only that there are problems you need to know about if you're planning to invest in them. As we said before, for the average reader of this book, they are the best tools you can have for building your portfolio. But by being aware of the potential pitfalls, you can set yourself apart from the average investor. That way, when you or your advisors get done sorting through the thousands of mediocre funds, you will have arrived at the cream of the crop.

The factors to consider with mutual funds can be numerous, but let us highlight the three most important: performance, fees and taxes.

During the1990s, only a very small percentage of mutual funds outperformed the S&P 500, and most mutual funds do not do even that well. When choosing funds to invest in, it is critical to look for ones that have been in the top 25% in performance over at least ten years. This should drop the available number of funds in each category significantly. If you are planning to work with a financial advisor, you should write that down as your number one criteria.

Now, let's move on to the subject of fees. Something wonderful about America is that when there is an opportunity to make money in a particular business, entrepreneurs flock to the opportunity. Remember hula hoops, Beanie Babies and Tickle-Me Elmo? If it's hot, you're sure to find plenty of people who want in. The same thing has happened in the mutual fund industry. The number of funds has exploded in recent years from a couple of thousand funds to well over 10,000. In fact, there are currently more funds available to the retail public than there are stocks traded on the New York Stock Exchange!

This rapid expansion of funds should send a message to the average investor: somebody is making money! There is major success to be had in mutual funds, whether from loaded funds or no-load ones. The fund company makes money, the salesperson makes money and the brokerage firm makes money.

But there are fees: expense ratios, 12b-1 fees and trading expenses. Expense ratios are the obvious fee that all mutual funds have, even no-loads—they go purely toward the expense of running the fund. These fees range from as low as .25% for index funds up to over 2.5% for some of the most expensive funds. The normal range is from .8% to 1.7%.

12b-1 charges are the fees that go to pay sales commissions and marketing. Approximately 1% is the typical annual fee for a mutual fund sold by a broker or an insurance agent. When a broker charges a load upfront, then the annual residual load is usually .25%.

Trading expenses come from the mutual fund turnover—the buying and selling of stocks inside of a mutual fund. This often adds up to approximately another 1.2% per year of invisible costs for the average fund. We say invisible because the fund companies do not have to report these costs, but trust us, they're there.

Let's add it all up: 1.4% for expense ratio plus 1% for the commissions, plus 1.2% for turnover expenses. This adds up to 3.6% per year for a great many mutual funds. Now, we know what some of our readers are thinking: "I own no-loads. And no-load means free." Not so fast! Even with no-load funds, the only expense that is absent is the 12b-1 fee. The rest of the fees still apply.

It is no wonder that so many mutual funds did not outperform the S&P 500 index in the nineties. It is hard to run fast with that kind of weight on your back. Judging by the fees we've looked at, many mutual funds start the year off at a 3.6% deficit to the S&P 500. That means managers have to outperform the market by over 3.6% *just to break even*.

So, the second thing to have written down when visiting a financial advisor or sifting through funds is that the *total* expense ratio should be less than 1.5%, and the turnover should be less than 100%. This will keep the expenses down to a reasonable level.

One option to consider is index funds. Index funds simply

replicate the fund they are tracking, so an S&P 500 index funds simply holds all the stocks in the S&P 500 in proportion to their market capitalization (the total value of these stocks). Index funds have very low fees because they are simple to manage— they don't require expensive portfolio managers to pick out stocks. Historically, index funds have outperformed most mutual funds, largely because of their lower fees. Vanguard is the largest and most reputable of the index fund companies.

Finally, we should take a look at the tax implications of investing in mutual funds. These can be *major*. It is estimated that between 1994 and 1999, investors in diversified U.S. stock funds surrendered an average of 15% of their annual gains to taxes. This is a staggering statistic for investors to consider if they own mutual funds in a taxable account.

That leads us to criteria number three: the funds that are acceptable must be tax-efficient. A good advisor will know which ones are tax-efficient, and if they do not know, it's time to find a new advisor. We address the topic of taxes on mutual funds in much more detail in the next chapter.

– CHAPTER 23 –
TAXES: THE SILENT KILLER

The power to tax involves
the power to destroy.

— Chief Justice John Marshall, 1819

Taxes are typically the largest or second largest expense most people have. For a high-income earner, taxes can eat up over half of their income. We probably don't need to tell you that. You see it every time your paycheck comes. But you should not assume that whatever you are paying right now is the smallest amount you *can* pay. We have seen articles recently in well-known publications showing that the majority of Americans are OVERPAYING their taxes. That's right! The IRS itself says that the majority of taxpayers are not taking full advantage of all of the tax breaks that are legally available!

This is not a book about taxes. This is a book about creating a vision for your life that is much bigger and more fulfilling than the one most people have for their lives. But you must choose between knowledge and ignorance; you must choose between action and inaction; you must choose between using the tax system to your advantage and being taken advantage of by the tax system.

It is a very real possibility that you are overpaying in taxes right now. There is even a chance that you could save enough each year in taxes to fund a large portion of your plan to make work optional. Think about that! What if you are currently overpaying the IRS enough money each year to fully fund your plan? We'll give you some general advice about being tax-aware, followed by some specific investment-related tax suggestions.

Rule 1: Hire a qualified tax advisor, preferably a certified public accountant.

We cannot stress too much the importance of having a CPA to help create a plan for reducing your tax burden down to the lowest legal level.

We have several trustworthy CPAs to whom we refer our clients to help them formulate a plan. It's important to understand the importance of not waiting until the end of March to start thinking about taxes. It should be an integral part of every person's financial strategy. The beauty of working with a CPA is that no knowledge of taxes is needed—they will help with the preparation and execution of your game plan.

If you have a financial advisor and a CPA who keep in consistent contact throughout the year, there is an even better chance that your investments will be tax-efficient and that you will end up keeping more of what you earn.

Rule 2: Maximize the contributions to company-sponsored retirement plans and personal IRAs.

We do not need to go into detail on all of the available options in this area or the funding limits for each type of plan. What we will say is this: these are the greatest gifts the government will ever give you.

Consider this: every time money is put into a qualified plan at work, the government is essentially matching the contribution by not taxing the money you put in. The money is still taxed when it is removed to be spent, but that will be fifteen or more years down the road after the money has grown without being taxed for fifteen years. It makes a big difference.

Let's look at how much of a difference this can make.

Let's say an employee puts $10,000 into their employer's plan and leaves it in there for fifteen years. If the money grows at an 8% average compound annual rate, they would have **$31,722**.

Let's say the same employee decides not to use their company's plan and invests the $10,000 on their own. Remember, they will have to pay taxes on the $10,000 now if they do not use their company-sponsored plan, so they are realistically investing $7,000, not $10,000. If the money could grow at 11% without being taxed, then it will probably only grow at 9% after taxes. Remember, in a taxable account taxes must be paid along the way, which means the returns suffer. So how much will the $7,000 grow at a compound annual growth rate of 9%? The ending balance after fifteen years will be only **$16,776**.

The difference is $14,946. The employee will have $14,946 more dollars to work with if they use the company-sponsored plan (or some other self-employed qualified plan if they work for themselves). This is very powerful and should be used to the full extent of the law.

We know what some people are thinking: "If I can't touch this money until I am fifty-nine and a half, how can I make work optional at forty-five or fifty years old?" Be not afraid! There are ways to get access to funds from a Retirement Plan before age fifty-nine and a half. You just have to know how to do it properly, without costing yourself the 10% penalty. This is where the use of a qualified financial advisor and CPA is very useful.

We suspect that not even the IRS understands all of the tax laws, so we are certainly not planning on trying to decipher them here. We are, however, committed to helping you avoid some of the most common tax mistakes that people tend to make—particularly the problems that can arise if you do not sift carefully through mutual funds to find those that are the most tax-efficient.

Let's look at an example to help illustrate how much taxes can set someone back on the way to Making Work Optional. A mutual fund that is not tax-efficient can easily cost you up to 25% of your gains. So, let's say that a mutual fund that you are considering has averaged 10% per year for ten years. There is a very real possibility that the after-tax returns would be 8% per year for a middle-income taxpayer.

If $10,000 is invested and grows at 10% for fifteen years, the money will grow to $41,772.

If $10,000 is invested and grows at 8% for fifteen years, the money will grow to $31,721.

Taxes could strip $10,000 off your total investment over a fifteen-year period.

It is important to note you do not have to pay the taxes on your mutual funds with money from the mutual funds. You can leave the money in the funds and pay the taxes with money from your normal cash flow. If you choose this path, your returns would still be 10%. However, you could be investing that money instead of sending it to Uncle Sam to pay the taxes on your mutual funds.

If you own mutual funds in a taxable account, we strongly recommend that you only own funds that specialize in tax-efficient investing. In these funds, the manager tries to offset any gains with losses and keeps the trading activity lower than in non-tax-efficient funds. This keeps the tax liability down.

There are companies that specialize in this form of investing. Two companies in particular are known for tax-efficient investing: Eaton Vance, which has actively managed mutual funds, and Vanguard, which has some very low-cost funds that try to reduce the tax bite (Vanguard calls these tax-managed funds). Both of these companies have been able to decrease the taxable distributions from their mutual funds drastically, especially in comparison to a non-tax-efficient variety.

One final useful tool is a variable annuity—a contract that allows you to invest in a number of investment portfolios and receive periodic payments starting at a specified future date. Please understand, variable annuities are not appropriate for every situation. Where we find them to be very appropriate is in situations where an individual is fortunate enough to have additional money to invest *on top of* their contributions to their company-sponsored retirement plan and personal IRA. We like them because the government allows money to grow inside of variable annuities without being taxed. You are only taxed when you withdraw the gains. It is important to remember that there are unique tax consequences to withdrawing money from a variable annuity, and there can be extra tax penalties if withdrawals are done inappropriately. But if used properly, a variable annuity can be used to accelerate the benefits of compounding interest without the drain of taxes.

CHAPTER 24

HOW TO FIND THE LAST FINANCIAL ADVISOR YOU'LL EVER NEED

He who can take advice is sometimes superior to him who can give it.

– Karl von Knebel

On the journey toward Making Work Optional, keep one very important fact in mind: it cannot be done alone! This is a personal journey—each person is ultimately responsible for its outcome in their lives—but no one will ever make it if they do not surround themselves with top-notch advisors. Very few people have enough time, energy and expertise to be well-versed in taxes, estate planning, insurance, investments, financial planning and everything you need to know to quickly and successfully make work optional.

Along with this need for top-notch advisors comes the need for long-lasting relationships. It is not enough to have a fantastic financial advisor if your relationship with them is not maintained over a period of many years. The hope and goal of any relationship with a professional advisor—be it a CPA, attorney or financial advisor—is that it last forever. If you change advisors every three years, it doesn't matter how good any new advisor is; you will already be locked into a pattern of constant turnover.

So the question is: How can you find an advisor you can trust? How can you find someone who not only will care about your financial situation, but who will also have the tools needed to pilot your financial ship safely into harbor?

The checklist you are about to read has been developed from interactions with hundreds of advisors, some world-class, some average and some just plain abysmal. Since our experience has been in the investment arena, this checklist is geared more toward investment advisors than CPAs, attorneys or other professionals. But regardless of the type of advisor you are looking for, these guidelines can serve as a starting point for finding the last financial advisor you will ever need.

1. Do they share your core values?

If you deeply value your faith and your advisor does not, your difference in opinion could be an eventual stumbling block. If you hold your family sacred and your advisor has very little sense of family, conflict is likely to occur. If you wish to invest in companies that practice ethics similar to yours, it's best to find an advisor who feels similarly. If you have great passion for Making Work Optional, and your advisor is content to wander through life without such a quest for financial freedom, you will most likely encounter major frustration in your relationship.

You want your advisor to see eye to eye with you—not just on investment selection, but on the reasons you are investing in the first place. It is not enough to agree on the *what* of your investments; there must also be agreement on the *why*. Any advisor gives their clients directions based not only on their investment knowledge, but on their core values as well.

Jenna received an inheritance and had questions about what to do with it. She knew she needed to make further retirement investments, but she also had credit card balances that she had carried for some time. She had managed to lower the balances substantially, but she still had quite a distance to travel before the balances reached zero. We shared her vision for being debt-free and understood the need to eliminate her credit card debt as quickly as possible. So while retirement investing was a priority for our client, the values both we and Jenna shared regarding debt reduction helped simplify the decision to first pay off the credit card debt and then invest the difference.

One pastor we worked with was preparing to receive a large insurance settlement for far more money than he had ever seen in his life. What the pastor pointed out, and what we were well aware of, was that he had a great passion for giving. He viewed this settlement as an opportunity to do an enormous amount of good for other people.

Instead of discussing options for setting up a portfolio that would provide the pastor with an income stream for the rest of his life, we looked at ways to set up a portfolio that would do the maximum amount of good for ministries, non-profits and individuals in need.

Because we shared similar perspectives on faith issues, we were able to work out solutions that were in sync with the pastor's core values. But what if the pastor worked with someone who did not share these values? Would the process take longer? Possibly. Would tensions arise if his advisor tried to suggest that the pastor take a more "traditional" approach and use the wealth for personal security and freedom? Probably. Would the pastor feel affirmed in expressing his vision for how the wealth should be used? Not likely.

Your advisor does not have to be a carbon copy of you in every philosophical, political, economic and religious category, but they should have similar core values.

When your advisor's values are in line with yours, you know you are being understood. You know you have someone in your corner who is fighting not just for your financial well-being, but for your deeply held beliefs about life as well.

2. **Do they hold an advanced investment designation? And do they have a systematic plan for growing in their investment knowledge?**

Most financial advisors must pass a series of tests to qualify as an advisor. These exams primarily test an advising hopeful on how financial markets function, the different investment instruments available and regulatory and ethical issues. What these exams *do not* teach is the ability to develop and manage a well-balanced portfolio. They do not teach principles of asset allocation, how to determine insurance needs or how to create a comprehensive financial plan.

The truth is that anyone with above-average intelligence, passable social skills and enough money to subscribe to the *Wall Street Journal* can become a financial advisor. Becoming truly outstanding at providing financial direction, however, takes far more than a Series 7, a phone, a call list and a computer.

A licensed advisor may have the authority to swing a financial hammer, but that does not necessarily mean you should give them free reign to remodel your financial home. Give someone the permission to build that addition simply because they are licensed, and you may come home to find 5-foot ceilings, no windows, uneven walls and a dirt floor.

Kevin, a former colleague of ours, shared with us the story of his very first interview upon entering the financial services industry. He went in armed with a number of questions for the branch manager. One of the questions he asked was, "Why do people fail in this business?" The primary explanation the manager gave was that advisors go into the business thinking they are analysts rather than salespeople. Confuse your role, he said, and you are sure to fail. He also commented that a truly good advisor was one who left the actual investing up to professional fund managers and concentrated on gathering assets for the firm.

While Kevin did not fancy himself an analyst, neither did he consider himself the financial equivalent of a bird dog—slogging through the marsh of cold call lists and white pages, hoping to retrieve only a few client accounts here and there.

The most amazing thing about Kevin's first foray into financial services was not the emphasis on sales. Sales are a very real part of the business. The ability to present information, communicate suggestions and help people make financial decisions is a necessary component of the industry; if their advisors lacked these skills, many clients would be left to make their own decisions without sufficient information, often to their detriment. The emphasis on sales is not what amazed us; it was that sales skills were emphasized *to the exclusion of and as a substitute for* investment knowledge.

As a matter of course, you should find an advisor who has pursued education beyond basic licensing—an advisor who thinks that their investment knowledge is just as important as their skill at sales. There are a number of investment designations that indicate an advisor's professionalism and competence. The Chartered Financial Planner (CFP™) is probably the most recognized financial planning designation. CFP™ training gives advisors specialized knowledge across a broad number of financial categories including investments, insurance, taxes and estate planning.

Other designations include the Chartered Financial Analyst (CFA), held by many mutual fund managers and Wall Street analysts, and the Chartered Financial Consultant (ChFC). Dozens of these designations are offered to advisors; do not hesitate to ask yours which designations they hold and what expertise they have because of the training.

In addition to official designations, an advisor should have a passion for expanding their base of investment knowledge. You want doctors who are on the cutting edge of medicine, CPAs who are up-to-date on the tax code and lawyers who are current on their area of law. It should be no different with a financial advisor. Ask your advisor what books they are currently reading or what continuing education they are pursuing. If they have an answer, they'll love to chat with you about what they're learning. If they don't have an answer, that should be a warning sign that they do not value ongoing growth and training. There are some people who, in terms of their careers, are just going through the motions. They are content just to punch the clock and collect a paycheck. They are not interested in growing and learning. They are not interested in doing an exceptional job. They are not interested in making a difference. They have mentally and emotionally checked out of their careers, and they are on the countdown to retirement. Is this the kind of person to whom you want to trust your financial future? Do yourself a big favor—find someone who cares enough about their clients and their career that they make learning a priority.

3. **Will they be able to create a personal financial plan for you that encompasses your entire financial situation, present and future?**

When we were children, all three of us loved playing backyard football. We all wanted to be the quarterback, and we all wanted to call the plays. If you have ever experienced the wonders of backyard football, you'll remember how the play calling went. Whoever was the designated quarterback that afternoon would huddle the team together, and with incredible precision and decisiveness, would call a play like, "Just go out and get open." Or the ever popular, "You go left, you go right, you go up the middle."

Bill's portfolio resembles this game of backyard football; it resembles a patchwork quilt more than a cohesive, purposeful collection of investments. There is no clear purpose in the portfolio. It has a little bit of everything—a little growth, a little value, a little large-cap, a little small-cap—but it lacks a consistent framework.

In addition to the problems with his investment portfolio, Bill has no idea how or even if his insurance needs are covered, he has questions about estate planning and he is beginning to worry about how well prepared he is to help his two daughters pay for college.

Bill doesn't simply need an investment advisor. He needs someone to help him gain clarity about his overall financial health. Make no mistake: not all financial advisors are financial planners. When choosing an advisor, make sure they are well trained across a broad spectrum of financial issues. This assures that as your needs change, you won't outgrow your advisor.

4. **Do you enjoy interacting with them on a personal basis?**

The goal is to have an investor-advisor relationship that will last for the rest of your life. You want to work with an advisor whom you connect with personally.

We all have difficult clients, high-maintenance relationships and hard-to-deal-with relatives. There are certain hard-to-deal-with people that we HAVE to interact with. But when you are choosing an advisor, you should make sure they are someone you like being around.

A great question to consider is, "Can I see myself working with this advisor for the next twenty years?"

5. **Does he have an established system for ongoing contact and follow-up?**

At the very least, you should meet with your advisor once a year for a portfolio or plan review. For more complex situations or during volatile markets, it may be appropriate to meet more often.

Before you commit to working with an advisor, make sure this is a regular part of their practice. If they do not have an established system for contact with their clients, don't make the mistake of believing they start with you.

These are the kinds of questions that any advisor

worth their salt should be willing and excited to answer. There may be other questions you would add to the list. The important point is that asking hard questions such as these needs to be an integral part of the process of finding an advisor you can work with in harmony and security.

– CHAPTER 25 –
CONCLUSION

Persistence is a great element of success. If you only knock long enough and loud enough at the gate, you are sure to wake up somebody.

– Henry Wadsworth Longfellow

A burning desire, clear goals and an intense focus are three of the most important prerequisites to success in any endeavor. But we also want to emphasize the importance of *enjoying* the journey to Making Work Optional.

It's important to not focus entirely on the end goal; one of the most frequent causes of unhappiness is an intense desire for something that one doesn't have. You will not suddenly become happy the day that work is optional if you have been unhappy along the journey. Happiness comes from appreciating what life has given you and working toward other experiences that life may have to offer. Learn to savor the lessons you will learn along the way. Be prepared to make mistakes and have setbacks. Very few people will make the entire journey without making an error or two. *We* all still make mistakes, and we are very well schooled in the areas of financial planning and investing.

Also, remember to be patient with your spouse and children. They may not catch on to the vision as fast or as intensely as you do.

Finally, pray for wisdom and guidance along your journey to Making Work Optional. This is a worthy task you are undertaking. It is one that will shape your family for generations to come. The values you will instill in yourself and your family are invaluable and will set you apart from the crowd for the rest of your life.

> *"Never, never, never, never give up."*
>
> – Winston Churchill